AF304954

Praise for *Art Is How God Loves Us*

"*Art Is How God Loves Us* is a radiant guide back to wonder and to the truth that our lives are works of art held in divine love. Drawing on her deep experience as a musician and coach, Dr. Merideth Hite Estevez weaves personal stories with a reverent, artful attention to the luminous within our lives. Here is a call to remember that we are, in every sense, *beautifully and wonderfully made.*"

—**Maria Bowler**, author of *Making Time: A New Vision for Crafting a Life Beyond Productivity*

"Part memoir, part spiritual guidebook, *Art Is How God Loves Us* is a gorgeous and deeply heartfelt look at our most important conversations: the ones we have with the Divine. How can we dance with creativity as we would with the Divine? Estevez shows us the way. Her insightful reflections on art are far-reaching and fascinating. Her deeply personal stories take readers around the globe and into her heart. She shows how the holy is illuminated through the art we encounter and the art we make ourselves. The book is filled with inspiring, playful exercises that invite any person—self-declared artist or otherwise—to deepen their relationship with themselves, the created, and the Creator. I'll be coming back to this book again and again!"

—**Heather Lanier**, author of *Raising a Rare Girl* and *Psalms of Unknowing*

"Merideth Hite Estevez invites us to a feast of poetry, paintings, and paying attention to all the ways God revels in God's creation. An awakening to ourselves and the world, this book is a love letter to the millions of ways God cares for us and enriches our lives with beauty."

—**Erin Hicks Moon**, cohost of the *Faith Adjacent* and *Shelf Respect* podcasts; *Publishers Weekly* bestselling author of *I've Got Questions: The Spiritual Practice of Having It Out with God*

"I was brought to tears multiple times while reading this book. Merideth Hite Estevez's words will break you open, leaving you teetering on the edge of heartache and joy. Her stories and lessons are uniquely hers and yet strangely familiar. *Art Is How God Loves Us* will unravel you, but whatever it tears down, Estevez rebuilds with hope and truth. This book is for every season, feast or famine, and for every person, artist or otherwise: because, as she highlights, each one of us is an artist in our own right—living and creating in abundance—if only we have eyes to see."

—**Jennafer Newberry**, Broadway actress

"With an artful weaving of intellect and intimacy, this book invites deep reflection and gentle transformation. Writing masterfully with warmth and disarming honesty, Merideth Hite Estevez has rekindled my spiritual imagination—both as a creator and as one who has known long-suffering—offering another tender thread of healing for my heart."

—**Kristin Vanderlip**, writer, artist, and founder of The Pen & Mend Collective

"For all of us frequented by the ghosts of achievement and the incessant pressure to prove our worth, this book is like a long-needed exhale. In *Art Is How God Loves Us*, Merideth Hite Estevez gently invites us to return to the joy of the created—where our songs, our words, our works can become sacred spaces for us to dwell together with God and to experience the vastness of his love in the here and now."

—**Sarah E. Westfall**, author of *The Way of Belonging*

ART IS HOW GOD LOVES US

The Sacred Beauty of Created Things

ART IS HOW GOD LOVES US

Merideth Hite Estevez

Broadleaf Books
Minneapolis

ART IS HOW GOD LOVES US
The Sacred Beauty of Created Things

Library of Congress Control Number: 2025951537 (print)

Cover image: Unsplash/Public Domain: Vase of Flowers,
Jan Davidsz de Heem, 1670
Cover design: Olga Grlic

Print ISBN: 979-8-8898-3645-2
eBook ISBN: 979-8-8898-3646-9

To the artists:
the pencil stealers, the orderers of
chaos, the writers of love letters.
And to Edwin, always.
Jesu Juva

God creates out of love, not necessity.

—Makoto Fujimura

Contents

Introduction: Art's Open Door
Frédéric Chopin, Andante Spianato (1834)

The melody cracked open a door I thought would be closed forever.

Terrified, I sat cross-armed in Mrs. Cox's ear-training class, waiting my turn. I stared down at the notes I was about to recite, headachy and frozen. I had stopped drinking coffee on ear-training days (M-W-F) because of the shaking, but that only helped so much. When Mrs. Cox asked me to stand and sing or count something, which was basically every class, I hid my trembling hands behind my back.

The fact that I had never learned Juilliard's specific ear-training method, "fixed do," (as in *do, re, mi*) sent me spinning into an intense shame spiral. I was in pursuit of my doctorate of musical arts, after all. Sure, I had a bachelor's, an artist diploma, and a master's of music—seven years of higher education and conservatory-level training—under my belt. Those degrees might as well have been in astrophysics as far as Mrs. Cox was concerned. Thus far in my education, we'd only used "movable do," so her class required me to sing in a whole new language. (Fixed or movable "do" are two different ways of teaching solfège or sight-singing, where each note is given a different syllable, à la *The Sound of Music.*) I walked into that course of study as a beginner, something I was (and still am) very much not good at being.

My experience in this class three times a week was proof that I didn't belong, that I didn't have what it took. My hair was immaculate, my outfit carefully curated, my perfectionist tendencies were neatly secured in my impossibly heavy backpack. This girl from Middle of Nowhere, South Carolina, walked the streets of New York City as an impostor.

On that day, I had reached the apex of anxiety, the moment we were to combine all we had learned for the entire semester in an exam: reciting a solo piece from our instruments' literature, singing it from memory in "fixed do" solfège in front of the entire class.

Next up, across the circle from me, was a pianist whom I had never heard speak a word to anyone. He stood, his dark eyes avoiding our gaze, rising with hesitance, one hand bracing his desk, and began to sing Chopin's *Andante Spianato.* His five-foot frame almost buckled at the weight of it. As a wind player, I immediately noticed how shallow and high his breathing was, the awkward pianistic melody so unnatural to sing with a human voice. His *si-re-mi-faaaaaa* was nasal but heartfelt, and his gentle eyes stared beyond the circle of classmates, never wavering. With clear pitch, he set down each note so tenderly, like shards of something precious and breakable.

Suddenly, the door cracked again, just a sliver of light broke through. Hearing that melody felt like meeting an old friend for the first time. It had a simplicity to it, soaring, but almost hymn-like with a tinge of melancholy. I knew the Italian words in the title: *Andante* means "walking speed," and *spianato* means "even" or "smooth." And these came through even in my classmate's amateur singing. The lyrical line was suspended in the air like a rock skipping across the water.

Instantly, tears welled in my eyes. Not stress or shame tears—I had hidden those kinds of tears in that fifth-floor classroom numerous times that semester—no, these were tears of joy. I let them fall down my face onto the music for my exam, Richard Strauss's *Oboe Concerto*, as a flare of some childlike curiosity sprang up so suddenly it stole my breath.

Hans Christian Andersen is widely quoted as saying, “Where words fail, music speaks.” I look back on that day at Juilliard and see that I was so deafened by my shame—my fear of not being good enough—that I stood mute and trembling, stuck and silent. The shame not only pushed me into myself and made me small, but I realize now, it also made me unable to hear music speak. Music, which had once led me beyond myself and into some big, wide world of hope and possibility, no longer sang to me because all I could hear was the roar of my own shame.

The performance of his exam—the gift of that melody he gave me, even clumsily—opened a door I thought had been locked long ago, a portal to beauty, curiosity, and faith. My shame evaporated as an overwhelming benevolence called me home.

At that moment, I fought a deep desire to run to the library and find the score and a piano, to experience what it felt like to make that tune come from a box of strings and hammers. Even though I was only slightly less inept at piano than I was at ear training, it wouldn’t matter. One line of that music, sung by a pianist in solfège while breathing “wrong” in an ear-training exam, struck a deep chord within my soul. It wasn’t about the quality of the performance. It was something beyond, something transcendent.

Why Music Moves Us

Recently, I read about a group of religious and spiritual contemplatives from across eight different traditions (Buddhist, Hindu, Jewish, Islamic, Native American, Russian Orthodox, Protestant, and Roman Catholic) who gathered in Snowmass, Colorado, in 1984 for what they called a “big experiment.” Led by Father Thomas Keating, they meditated together and then gathered to discuss. They quickly realized that while the words they used to explain or quantify their experiences differed, the experiences themselves were similar.

In the years following these meetings, Father Keating presented the group with Eight Points of Agreement, which were edited and revised. Two of those agreements provide words that help me understand what I experienced that day at Juilliard, and many times since:

No. 1: "The world religions bear witness to the experience of Ultimate Reality, to which they give various names."
No. 6: "Ultimate Reality may be experienced not only through religious practices but also through nature, art, human relationships, and service to others."

Although I couldn't have articulated it at the time, when I heard Chopin's *Andante Spianato* in the timid voice of my ear-training classmate, it was Ultimate Reality that broke down the door and beckoned me to enter.

Today, I might reach for words like *God* or *Spirit* to describe it, but back then, the faith of my childhood was barely breathing under the suffocating need to be perfect, drowning in my self-hatred and crippling insecurities.

On that day, Ultimate Reality sang to me—in solfège, believe it or not—and it was a miracle. I somehow recognized a melody I had never heard before. Like a song sung to a child, it glowed with familiarity, mutuality, and Love—a tender memory of something beautiful that I couldn't quite remember.

Music, at that moment, was no longer a criterion but a communion. It required nothing of me but my attention, which was everything.

Tender Strength

I had not heard creativity's deeply spiritual invitation to joy all those years ago at Juilliard, or even before that, if I am honest. I think that I was doing the thing that artists (or all of us) do when fear or shame shows up: We shut the door to spiritual experience out of self-protection. The competition and judgmentalism, not only of the schools or studios I was in but of the work environment within my very own mind, were toxic. Subconsciously, I avoided Ultimate Reality because I expected God to judge me, too.

But I know now that when we shut ourselves off from each other and from something larger than us, we also shut out the possibility of joy. In the "thick skin, tender-hearted" life of an artist, many think it is the thick skin that artists need to cultivate most, that the tender heart is a given. But in my experience, a tender heart can be so easily hardened by fear and shame, by life. And sometimes, the tenderest hearts construct the toughest armor.

Tenderness is a dangerous thing for an artist to lose.

For so long, my sensitivity seemed like a liability. If I just had more confidence, didn't take everything so personally, if my heart was an impenetrable fortress of creative control, if I could stop caring so much about what people thought—then I'd be happy. Then I'd "make it."

But through the song that moved me that day, Ultimate Reality snuck in through a crack in the armor I'd built around my tender heart and opened it wide.

And so, before you read any further, artist or not, I want to warn you. If you want to tame your tenderness, to cut off the vulnerable parts of yourself that could be hurt or disappointed or judged, if you want to avoid the presence or existence of a Higher Power, then best not listen to music at all.

Don't hold a toddler in your arms.

Refuse to look west at dusk.

Decline that invitation to your friend's art show.

Don't ever find yourself in the same room as Michelangelo's towering *David* or a canvas of Vincent van Gogh.

Don't take a long, meandering drive in October across northern Michigan.

Don't read stories, true or fictional.

Avoid the study of sea turtles, who somehow swim five thousand miles back to the beach where they were born.

Run out when the theater gets dark.

Above all, keep so busy that you manage to never feel your feelings.

Hold others to the impossibly high standards to which you hold yourself and never stop striving.

Lock your heart away from beauty and art so that it will never break.

Because there is a spiritual song that created things sing, and your heart knows the refrain. When we experience beauty, human-made or natural, it is the Creator who has left the door cracked between Ultimate Reality and this one.

Whisper-Shout

Maybe you're wondering what I did with this spiritual encounter under the fluorescent lights of a Juilliard classroom. I wish I could say that it gave me the strength to forgive myself for the ways I had "failed," or to be more gentle with myself as I was learning, or to love music again after years of wondering if I should quit—but in reality (painfully lower case and very much not ultimate), I didn't have the courage yet to loosen my grip. After another week of hand-wringing and panic, I somehow managed to pass Ear Training with a B minus (another miracle). I wandered the streets of New York with that Chopin tune in my headphones, longing to find the thin place again.

Within weeks, my shame sealed up the crack in my heart's armor, and I passed the whole thing off as a strange but ultimately insignificant occurrence. I wasn't ready to walk through art's open door yet.

The memory of that day in class reminds me that perfectionism always slams shut my heart and locks the deadbolt.

It reminds me that Ultimate Reality sings, not only under the spotlights of the recital hall with superb acoustics on a ten-foot Steinway with a professional pianist at the keyboard but also through the rattly voices of recitation exams, shallow breathing, leaky oboe reeds, and (in the stories of my faith tradition) smelly shepherds and bleeding women.

It reminds me that we busy ourselves with the work of being "good enough" so we feel like we are the kind of people who deserve to experience beauty or feel joy, when all along, it was Beauty and Joy that were seeking us. They sing a song that, on some atomic level, we already know. It is just a matter of listening long enough to recognize it, to sit down and try to join in, however imperfectly it may come out.

At the intersection of art and faith, of creativity and spirituality, is an outstretched hand. It is calling on you to go next, not to perform but to simply attend, to listen, to join in when you feel ready. There's no need to be nervous because, while it includes you, it isn't a test of your readiness or worthiness.

It is more than an invitation, I implore you: *Please stop ignoring or pushing away these moments of beauty and connection in the busyness and noise of this reality. You were made for more.*

It whisper-shouts, *Look. Listen. Stay tender.*

It isn't a pointing teacher scrutinizing your recitation or a hard-hearted God who is disappointed in your lack of talent or skill, but rather, it is Love bidding you enter into the music that's been ringing since creation began.

Spiritual Synesthesia

After a certain age, music made my grandmother weep so intensely that church was out of the question. "O Lord, My God, When I, in Awesome Wonder," brought her to her knees. "Amazing Grace," even on the out-of-tune organ in the tiny

Ohio Evangelical United Brethren chapel, opened a wound so tender that she would have to slip out of the back alone and retreat to her car. I never asked her about it, and now, I never will on this side of heaven.

As a professional musician, I long to know what that music meant to her. As far as I knew, she came to faith in adulthood—those songs were not remembrances from youth. I want to believe it wasn't just grief that moved her in the familiar lilting rhythms of chorus-verse-chorus but also joy. I don't want to see this little anecdote, now that she's gone, as a failure to cope or the early signs of dementia that would eventually take her life. I choose to believe that in that music, she heard something deeper. Each plagal cadence, which sounded to us like an *Amen* of minimal effort, to my grandmother, sounded like love, like heaven itself.

Some people see colors when they hear music or taste a flavor when they see specific shapes. Synesthesia means that a single stimulus triggers multiple senses. What if my grandmother had a spiritual synesthesia brought on by that music, two radio wires crossed in her heart? We heard a volunteer choir, but she witnessed an overwhelming soundscape rich with love and meaning. And she couldn't take it.

I heard a story once about a pastor who, after a tragedy, stalked the streets desperately seeking God's presence. Night and day, he longed to see proof that God was with him. He said, "One day, in the city of New York—oh, what a day!—I cannot describe it, I seldom refer to it; it is almost too sacred an experience to name . . . I can only say that God revealed himself to me, and I had such an experience of his love that I had to ask him to stay his hand." My grandmother wasn't the only one who ran weeping from such experiences of love.

It doesn't say in that pastor's account what he was doing besides walking when God's presence rushed in, but I have no doubt some created beauty was involved. Through a painted sky or a burning bush, an Artist God seeks us. Author Anne

Lamott's conversion story begins with the hearing of a gospel choir singing from an open church window across the street from a flea market. Creation groans, but it also sings. Every created thing calls to us of God's love, vibrating with a mysterious spiritual song that, when we are willing to listen, we recognize.

Many years after my spiritual experience in the hallowed halls of Juilliard, I found a simple sentence in Makoto Fujimura's *Art and Faith: A Theology of Making*, a truth so resonant and freeing that I could barely believe it. If I could sum up the thesis of this book in seven words, I would borrow these: "God creates out of love, not necessity," or my translation: Art is how God loves us.

This volume is an invitation to experience this love of Ultimate Reality, through both sacred and secular, God and human-created things: art. We will use art as a lens through which to reflect deeply, experience our innate worthiness, and grow in faith. I will offer you tools to listen to, view, or experience the art all around you, and I will attempt to put into words a few moments where I, too, have prayed for God "to stay his hand." I imagine, if you've picked up this book, you have stories from your own life like this, and if not, I hope that you will leave behind any insecurity or intimidation you may have around art and let the sacred beauty of created things break open your life, to let the love of God sing through.

Rumors of the Real

In her book *Field Notes for the Wilderness*, Sarah Bessey shares a story of a spiritual experience she had at the Met Museum in New York. Not an art connoisseur, the extent of her knowledge of oil painting begins (and ends), she says, with the print of Claude Monet's "Water Lilies" purchased from her college bookstore. But one day in New York, she stumbled into the Met and stood before her first real van Gogh.

"Look at it, it's so beautiful," she thought. "It's really real. Van Gogh did this work and here it is and here I am and it's really real." She stood in the museum, and she wept.

She writes, "I had heard rumors that the real things were astonishing, but they were just that—rumors. All of my knowledge fell away in that instance of knowing: sure, here's a timeline and here are the influences and here are the patrons and the historical context and cheap posters, but . . . but what really mattered was the reality." She is awestruck by the difference she can feel from being in the same space with the original work, so much more real than the copies she'd seen in books.

This prompts a spiritual revelation. She writes, "Perhaps someday we will simply be before Jesus the way I stood before van Gogh's paintings in that gallery." Bessey realized that all the representations of Jesus that she had seen in the practice of her religion were as much the real Jesus as a printed poster from a bookstore was a real van Gogh. They spoke of the real thing, but they were not it. That doesn't diminish the representations but emphasizes the nature of art—the incomprehensible power of the Ultimate Reality to which it owes its being.

Art moves us because it speaks of the Really Real. The creation power embedded in every work of art, its hue and texture—these are just rumors, whispers of a truer Beauty, a deeper Reality that can only be made complete in God.

How to Read This Book

This book explores the personification of God as creative, naming the intersection of art and Artist, an invitation to consider art as a spiritual gateway. Each chapter engages with a specific work of sacred or secular fine art by those that Western culture calls "masters," as well as underrepresented creators of our time—artists of color, women, and Indigenous voices. You will be invited to view and interact with paintings and poems, symphonies, and sculptures. I invite you to make space to experience them however you can, whether through reproduction or recording (you will find a QR code at the back of the book that will lead you to a web page with all the art in one place) or—my preferred way: *live* and in person. These discussions of works of human art are interwoven with short prose-poem interludes inviting you to seek, wonder, and reflect on the themes from each part.

This exploration unfolds in three parts. Part I awakens our innate spiritual spark, urging us to engage with the world as the cosmos-shaping energy does: to see, order, listen, and hang on to the thread of creative calling. Part II reveals art as a companion in darkness, offering a sanctuary to voice our doubts, embrace uncertainty, and release our grip. The final part illuminates how a spiritual perspective on art guides us toward our Creator and our most authentic selves, as we begin to see life as poetry, embrace abundance in our gifts, and exchange fear for freedom.

Along the way, you will learn tools for engaging with art through a spiritual lens, something I call "Ars Nova," a Latin term used throughout history to denote art moving in a new direction. You will be invited to a deeper noticing, a divine hearing and seeing. You'll learn the first question I ask when encountering art in nature or on a museum wall. These new ways of being will slow you down and help you notice the volume of God's presence in your life. Lastly, we'll explore how your belovedness as a work of art yourself—God's craftsmanship, handiwork, *poem*—not only frees you from the pain of shame and fear but calls you to create. This way of being has transformed how I approach creation, creating, and created things. It has brought me a little closer to Reality after hearing of its rumors for years.

I share many of my vulnerable, personal stories throughout the book. I have changed most names and identifying details to protect the privacy of those involved. These stories are based on my memories of events, with the occasional creative license taken to bring the stories to life. The chapters and sections are in an intentional order, but they also stand alone if you'd like to jump around. I invite you to find a space and allow yourself time to experience the works of art and prompts before beginning to analyze them. To go deeper, use the study guide and devotional on your own or with others in your spiritual community.

I have greatly benefited from naming the source of creative inspiration, Ultimate Reality, as something outside of myself, and I call that force Spirit or God. My faith has always felt more like a trampoline than a brick wall, thanks to my spiritual teachers and mothers and fathers of the faith. Yet, words fail us when we use our limited human brain to describe divine things. I write from my perspective as a white Christian female born in the United States, and member of the Presbyterian Church (USA). We may not share specific doctrinal beliefs. We likely express our faith differently. I am humble enough to know we may not always agree. God exists outside of gender, and, while my personal journey has, for most of my life, involved using "He/Him" pronouns for God—a reflection of the traditions I grew up with—I embrace a more expansive understanding of the divine. My hope is to honor both the rich tapestry of spiritual tradition and the boundless nature of God, who transcends all human categories. So whenever possible, I look for the most invitational ways to explore spiritual themes; I trust you to take what is helpful and leave the rest.

In my online creative community, Artists for Joy, we have explored what we believe about the nature of the universe, each sharing openly about their experiences of the spiritual. I have seen Western and Eastern traditions intersect; Jews, Muslims, Christians, Agnostics, Buddhists, and more stand on the common ground of the transcendent nature of creativity and share their unique understanding of art. Like Father Keating and the others who created the Eight Agreements, I hope that the openness of those interfaith conversations comes through. May this book be a starting point for going deeper into your specific expression of faith or spirituality.

In a noisy world, my prayer for you as you begin this book is that you'll stay in the pew when the music moves you. That you'll stop at the world's open windows and listen to the gospel choir. That you will let the tears flow as you sense the dance between grief and joy that characterizes any encounter with the Real. I pray that you will seek God through art and find God seeking you, loving you, before time existed and here in the eternal now.

On second thought, may you leave the pew, get up, and join in.

Prelude
Redefining Art

How I sound on my instrument depends entirely on a finicky and temperamental plant, of all things. That is too generous—the fiber we use to make oboe reeds is technically a weed. I was always told that the best *Arundo donax* for oboists and bassoonists grows in Mediterranean France, but this invasive and fast-growing crop can survive in almost any soil or climate. In school, I meticulously sorted the tubes of cane using a small gauge; this is where the long process of reed-making begins, with the judging of many small, yellow, nature-made stalks. After spending $90 to $200 on a pound, I gasped when my teachers urged me to throw most of it away. If it presented any imperfections—if the bark was pale, white, or dull; if it had grooves or corrugations, the tell-tale gray air pockets; if it felt stringy or holey, like shredded wheat—it would land weightlessly in the trash without ceremony. Mother Nature wasn't interested in perfection, yet, by the light of the reed desk, we sought perfectly curved, goldilocks-level hard, thick-walled, immaculately straight, creamy yellow, and impossibly dense... weeds.

If that sounds ridiculous, it's because it is. Yes, you can simply buy them ready to use, and yet we serious oboists know that nothing anyone else makes will ever be good enough for us.

There are a dozen more tools and machines and intricate, seemingly esoteric steps needed to turn the tube cane into a working reed. If any of the measurements are off by a few hundredths of a millimeter, the reed will not work. And yet, at one point in my life, those weeds determined my entire sense of self-worth.

The Point of Personhood

It is easy to think, when we are in the thick of artistic training or when faced with the banal and persistent technicalities of everyday life, that this is all there is to being human, that subduing the chaotic forces that prevent perfection is our ultimate goal. The kitchen counters need wiping; the tops of the bookcases are dusty again. The receipt you've kept since 2012 for "tax purposes," the endless miscellaneous junk from the last time you moved—these invasive species have taken over your garage. The tyranny of dust and dirt, the pyramid scheme that is owning a home and filling it with things: If we aren't careful, we may think that handling these headaches is the essence of personhood, like I once thought reed-making was the essence of being an oboist.

Truth is, this pursuit of the technical over the experiential—which is to say, the spiritual—can distract us from what matters most: the joy inherent in creating a life in the first place. The weight of all that we carry—the deep desire to have more control, the endless pursuit of *better*—hunches us over and chains us to a proverbial desk and prevents us from doing the far more important work of *living.*

In life-managing and reed-making, when we miss the joy in the process, we risk making our striving the point. We mistake the means for the end, we value product over process, forgetting what it is that we are striving *for.*

And when we do that, we walk right past the spiritual invitation of creativity.

What Is Art

The etymology of the word *art* comes from the Latin *ars* which signified anything related to skilled labor. A goldsmith's work, for example, was deemed art because of the training and technique it demanded.

Art (with a capital *A*) means something specific to you, I'm sure. Maybe the word communicates a hierarchy, a world you belong to, or don't. It can convey elitism, pressure, and even trauma. I know from almost a decade of leading a community for creatives that *art* and *artist* can be loaded words, bringing memories of mean-spirited teachers and cold museums where we were unwelcome. I cannot count how many conversations I have had with readers and podcast listeners who start off by saying, "I am not an artist, but . . ." Some of us hold *art* and *artist* at arm's length because of disappointment, fear, or impostor syndrome, usually disguised as reverence or respect.

For so long, I thought art was synonymous with skill, that the quality of the art was directly proportional to the skill of the artist. And by those standards, my music, my reeds, my art, was never good enough because *I* was never good enough.

But what if the quality of the art depends, not on my skill, but on the animating force of something greater than me?

As long as we define art in connection with the skills we must cultivate or the products we must make, we will live in perpetual disappointment and anxiety. And even more importantly, we do not let ourselves be guided.

A New Definition

I'd lived too long enslaved to a false definition of art that demanded perfect technical skill and left no room for joy or wonder. What if, instead of some tool to measure how good or bad we are, art is simply *A*toms *R*esponding to *T*ranscendence?

Whether created with paint on a canvas, notes on a page, or chips in a marble block, all ART starts with the basic building blocks of the universe: atoms. My old definition held that art emerged when we added skill to those atoms. And yet, almost any artist will tell you that the whole of their creative effort equals more than the sum of its parts. From the humble and unremarkable tools of pigment and pounded wood, reed and wind, earth and water worked into clay. . . in the ARTist's hands, things come forth that we cannot explain.

ART is more than the product of skilled labor or the execution of some apprenticed technique. It is the building block of life itself, evidence of the creation power embedded in every atom, scattered like the stars of the Milky Way, glowing with recognition in the hands of the human ARTist, responding to the transcendent nature of the Really Real. ART is work of a Creating Spirit calling every atom into the deeper spiritual reality we might call transcendence. When we peer at it through this spiritual lens, any created thing becomes ART.

The impact of ART has little to do with the intentions, ideologies, or skill of the ARTist. It is not constrained by those things. This explains how works created for secular purposes can speak beyond their original connotation and vibrate with Love. If you're awake to the world, you have felt the presence of something beyond yourself in Johann Sebastian Bach's *St Matthew Passion* or in George Frideric Handel's *Messiah*, regardless of your faith background. Chills from Pablo Picasso's *Guernica*, that delightful sense of smallness and wonder while standing below Michelangelo's *David*—we feel this inexplicable *something* through fine art, yes, but also sense it in bird songs and crashing waves. *A*toms *R*esponding to *T*ranscendence—this definition explains how a sunset breaks us open, how a downpour cleanses and brings renewal, how a woolly bear caterpillar or a river teaches us something about living.

The very first verb of Genesis 1, the inciting action of God in my faith tradition, is *creating*, of all things—God making ART.

That creative catalyst continues to glimmer inside creation today. The wind against your skin, witnessing the very first smile of a brand-new person, the smell of the dish that means you are home, the clarity and joy of Wolfgang Amadeus

Mozart—at their atomic level, these creations call to something deep within us because they are responding to the energy present at creation; they are ART.

You Are an Artist

Maybe you are standing amid the wreckage of your creative dreams, and this all sounds a bit too intangible. Maybe you are in the "relentless pursuit of better" phase of your life or career, and you really wish the atoms you are currently wrestling with at the easel, reed desk, or computer would respond already to this transcendence I speak of. Maybe you would never use the title "Artist," with a capital *A*.

I do not claim to understand the mysteries of the Really Real, but I do know that believing that my art is not, at its core, a measure of my personal worthiness but a participation in the eternal and effortless dance of all creation—this heart shift has completely transformed my life.

We are atoms, too, remember. And something in us knows the way forward. Like a ripple across the water, like a sound wave through a reed, when we let ourselves connect to the spiritual gateway that creativity offers us, we can let ourselves be guided, not by our own strength but by a deeper, more powerful force than we can even grasp.

You are an ARTist because you are creating a life. We are all made of and work with the messy, beautiful, irreplaceable, and invaluable Atoms that Respond to Transcendence. There is no technique you need to master, no perfect product you need to make before you get into the club. It is something you *already are*. Accepting that calling—that reality—with a whole heart not only frees you from the fear of claiming the title and the tyranny of having to "make it," it also allows for the creative act to become a vehicle for your own personal discovery, healing, and true communion with God.

The Best Is Yet to Come

After much gnashing of teeth, years of self-hatred, and a decade of near-constant fretting, I've figured out how to make reeds that work for me. Even still, some days, the weeds win. But now, I know that the miracle of creation vibrates from a pulsing bass note of the Creator and, therefore, so does the oboe reed. This means I can work toward improving whatever craft I may feel called to, without the results comprising my value as a person, because *it doesn't ultimately depend on me.*

And, even when it is going well, I remember that, if what Sarah Bessey felt at The Met is true—if all the wonder and miracles of human creation in this realm are only rumors of something Really Real—then the best reeds, the best ART, is yet to come.

May you give yourself grace as you live in the land of "already and not yet" and see even the rumors of the Real as the miracle-gift they are. Responding to the call of transcendence with every atom, we can trust that our surrendering work will, in the end, restore and not destroy us.

As the Hebrew prophet Isaiah said of the Messiah—arguably the best news of perhaps any religious writing ever penned for the oboist—when we do stand before the Messiah, we can trust that "a bruised reed he will not break."

ARS NOVA

Let Art Be Light

When you encounter a work of art, human-made or natural, the following questions invite you into a spiritual dialogue. If you have training in the arts, you may need to consciously disengage your critical mind/eye and tune into your heart.

1. *What do you notice about the work of art?*
   Before you analyze, notice the art in front of you deeply. Give it your complete and undivided attention.

Even if you have seen this work before, name what you notice today. There is no wrong answer. Be specific. No detail is too small. (This is the first question I ask when I stand before a work of art!)

2. *What are you carrying with you into this moment?* Now, turn your attention to yourself. Name what you bring with you to this art viewing session. Stress? Fear? Anxiety? Pain? Joy? Resist the temptation to fix or problem solve, simply be present to all you carry.
3. Imagine the work of art is a spark, a match struck in a dark room. *What does this work of art illuminate? How is Ultimate Reality speaking here and now? How would you like to respond?*

Part I

Spark

It doesn't interest me if you believe
in the God of my understanding or yours.
I want to know if you've stood weeping
before a painting,
if you've found the world of a novel more palatable
than this one.
I want to know if you've woken in the night
to the answer,
if rush of word or image or interval
doused the flames of overthinking
while you washed the dishes.

The Greeks said, "Eureka!"
(I have found it)
but I want to know if *One* has found you,
if the music makes you feel less alone.
I want to know if you've sensed
some overwhelming goodness
behind the color of the sky
or in the way baby hair wisps upward
along the back of her neck.
Have you ever wondered if your tenderness
makes you weak

or if it's this fierce surrender to Love
that makes us strong?

In every creation
there glows a glint in recognition of an Artist God.
The studio door slightly cracked,
a remnant, a spark of
Let There Be Light,
an inextinguishable pilot burns, still flickering.

I have been told, in that beauty, art sings a refrain
every heart knows.

—After David Whyte's poem "Self-Portrait"

Chapter 1

The Artist Sees
Vincent van Gogh, Olive Trees (1889)

Art is the highest form of hope.

—Gerhard Richter

The walls inside the corridor where I would wait for my oboe lessons had tactile wallpaper—small ridges of linen in off-white. Once a week, I would come early to stand in front of a door at the end of a passageway, awkwardly holding my fully assembled instrument, lesson notebook, water bottle, reed case, and all my bags strapped across my body like a music-major scarecrow. We were required to enter with everything already unpacked. I rocked on my heels like I was waiting for a train door to open, afraid to miss it. Sometimes, when I was very early, before unpacking, I would lean against the wall and feel the veins of that earthy, ancient wallpaper across my forehead. From that angle, I really saw it. The sheets didn't quite line up. It was starting to brown and peel. I ran my hands along the concrete clothed in linen like I was making a snow angel.

In those moments, that deteriorating corner of the world and I were kindred. We were both waiting for someone to tell us all the ways we were wrong.

Wonder Evaporated

I lost faith in many things in music school, not the least of which was God. The concept of a playful and loving Creator of the Universe that I had latched on to as a child had been replaced with a soul-deep cynicism. I only needed God insomuch as God could help me be the best oboist in the studio at Juilliard. In truth, I rarely thought of spiritual matters at all. I thought of how much I practiced and whether I was good enough and living up to my "potential."

In music theory class, when they'd show us the mastery of Ludwig van Beethoven's piano sonatas, my eyes would widen with wonder. For a moment, I'd sense the presence of something bigger. I'd feel that longing to believe. But later in the library, the wonder evaporated as I took apart that sonata note-by-note and put it back together for the assignment. However beautiful the sound might be, inside a hall without reverb, it will not resonate.

Then, what felt like all of a sudden, I began noticing this disturbing and persistent itchiness in my soul on my walk home from the practice rooms at night. The prayers I would utter later to my ceiling were ones of desperation: *Let me master the music. Let my reeds work. Let me be more talented, thinner, prettier. Let me be loved. Let me know I belong.* If I awoke the following day feeling better and saw how to push the feelings of unworthiness away by achieving something, these prayers felt petty, silly.

That is, until I reached the moment when even the biggest "atta girls" did not work anymore. The "successful" lessons or the well-played concerts no longer gave me the hit of happiness or validation they once did. Life felt hollow and pointless. Soon, even my previously rock-solid work ethic began to crack at the foundation. I could no longer motivate myself to practice or care. I watched myself go through the motions of music student life, a silent movie in black and white. I was spiritually adrift, alone on a raft in a treacherous sea of self-loathing.

Why I Abandoned God

In his 1963 essay, "The Seeing Eye," C. S. Lewis fielded questions about whether we would encounter God in space:

> You wouldn't relate to God the way a person on the first floor relates to a person on the second floor . . . You don't find God by going higher up in your own space. If God is our Creator, then we would relate to God as Hamlet would relate to Shakespeare. Now, how would Hamlet ever know anything about Shakespeare? Hamlet's not going to find him anywhere on stage. The only way he's ever going to meet him is if Shakespeare writes himself into the play.

God as Shakespeare. God as playwright. God as artist. My view of God back then couldn't have been more opposite.

For me, God had become a committee I felt I needed to impress. Father, Son, Holy Spirit, the Trinity Tribunal—their primary purpose being judgment. I looked at God through the lens of my own perfectionism, my belief that I had to be excellent to be loved. And while my childhood faith had helped me see the Tribunal as benevolent (just like most of my teachers were), conservatory life had emptied me. I had no more of myself to give away. That fall at Juilliard, I realized I had abandoned God because I thought I would need to earn the Tribunal's love, admiration, and praise—and I couldn't do it anymore.

Lenses

Imagine yourself wearing glasses with tinted, polarized lenses that make sunsets richer and the noonday sun palatable. When you wear them, they color everything you see. Lenses can protect our eyes, but to some extent, they mute or alter the world from its truest form.

What lenses are you wearing that color your view of God? What deeply held beliefs, positive or negative, inform how your brain puts language and image to things that can only be experienced spiritually?

In her book *The Artist's Way*, Julia Cameron explores how to recover a joy for creative expression by examining our "God concept." She asks, "How is the way you view God serving your creative expansion?"

Back then, the lens through which I saw God was anything but expansive. My *God concept* was what I now call "The Fault Finder."

What might yours be named? Sometimes, it is easier to see in hindsight. Look back on a time when you struggled with your faith and name the lens. Wrathful Dictator, Abusive Father, Disinterested Deity—these are a few I've heard from others.

Shakespeare Loved Hamlet

One day, after a particularly difficult lesson, when I felt myself turning toward a numbness that deeply frightened me, I decided I was done staring at walls and ceilings. Instead, I decided to go outside and look at the stars. I left my apartment on the Upper West Side and turned toward the park. I shook with desperation as I climbed a rock on the edge of the 86th-Street entrance. I lay down and stared at the sky, my eyes looking for God in heaven, and I sobbed.

I prayed, *If you are really up there—or everywhere—and you did make all this, then why don't you come down here and fix it. . . fix ME?*

And that's when my heart broke open, and I met the Artist God. A heavy, wet breeze blew against my back like a hug—or maybe more like a push. And as I heard the leaves of Central Park's trees submit to the Spirit and sensed the cold granite under my quivering legs, I knew that God did make all this. And if that was true, God made me, too. The sky glowed deep navy, and even with all the light pollution, the stars glimmered with a hope I'd never seen inside the city. I knew that I was speaking to a fellow artist, to my Artist.

Shakespeare must have loved Hamlet, as indecisive, melancholy, and complicated as he was: After all, he gave him more lines than any other character he penned in his entire lifetime. Could God love me like that?

The painter Gerhard Richter said, "Art is the highest form of hope." Put another way, creating is hoping with your hands. I knew what it was to hope so intensely, to believe in the material's power to create something beyond myself. I knew what it was to knit together the delicate sounds I was making from my instrument, to believe there was beauty in them, even when they failed to sound like I'd imagined they would. I knew what it was to care so intensely that you are willing to work for hours (or days) on one phrase, on two notes—unwilling to give up because there's a song in your heart that you long to sing.

I suddenly knew that it was God who'd put that song in my heart. Everything I had was God's. I could no longer take credit for how I had succeeded or fault for how I'd failed. That night in Central Park, I fell into the arms of the Author of everything beautiful I had ever loved. Someone who had read the same books and treasured the same music, who loved me like only an artist can, with passionate longing for what this world could be, for what I could be, for what I already was.

The Olive Trees

In 1889, Vincent van Gogh committed himself to an asylum in the south of France to be treated for mental illness. Initially, they confined him to a single chamber while offering him a makeshift painting studio in the room next door. I imagine him there, alone and waiting, feeling the wall against his forehead, too. Eventually, though, he was given run of the hospital grounds, and it was there that he found the subject of as many as fifteen paintings: olive trees.

In a letter to his brother Theo, he said he was "struggling to catch them . . . with their gold and silver, sometimes with more blue in them, sometimes greenish, bronzed, fading white above a soil which is yellow, pink, violet-tinted orange."

He went on to say that the "rustle of the olive grove has something very secret in it . . . immense. It is too beautiful for us to dare to paint it."

And yet he did dare. He dared fifteen times. He painted those trees in every season and time of day. With women among them picking their harvest and the dark Alps in the background. He evoked their blowing in the Provence wind, his brush heavy with paint, his signature strokes, one by one, over and over working out the shame and isolation of his own inner twisted trunk.

If creation is God's masterpiece, God loves and works on us like van Gogh with his mysterious olive trees. When you hear the artist describe them, you know they are truly seen: greenish bronze, fading white, yellow, pink, violet-tinged orange.

How would it shift your lens to see yourself as a song that God longs to sing? To see yourself as a beloved work of art to which God continually returns with hope and even joy?

Something I love about my faith tradition is that we know God is an artist who cares so much for creation, God wrote God's own self into the play. God self-discloses, enters stage right, comes in weakness and vulnerability, and is known in Jesus. Why? All so that we would know how deeply loved we are.

Seeing God as an artist—as the Artist—was the bridge I walked back to faith. I still wrestle with my Creator on walks in the woods or under the stars. Artist and art walking together, fourth wall broken, I bring all my doubts and fears—and the Artist, gently loving with compassion and grace, calls me to change. Not as a judgmental faultfinder but as a master potter, hands covered in clay. Never giving up, never ceasing to see my belovedness in the dirt.

To Be Seen Is to Be Loved

In the Hebrew Scriptures, Hagar calls God "El Roi," or "the God who sees" (Genesis 16). God sees you in every light—on stage and when no one's watching, in seasons of harvest and bare branches, inside the breakdowns and breakthroughs. You might feel like the faded, peeling wallpaper in a forgotten corridor, but the Artist God loves you enough to paint another and then another iteration. Through it all, God finds you a worthwhile and worthy subject. Not just worthy but immense, almost too beautiful to paint, something to return to again and again, to pursue with the precise effort and gentle tenderness of a Master Painter's brush.

Every creation holds something of the Artist within it. Art is God's creative power in action, and every created thing sings with the love of an Artist who sees.

Art is God hoping with God's hands.

The Artist's Eye

The verdict is in. You are good enough. At creation, God called you "very good." In Celtic spirituality, this was named the "original blessing." Not because of something you did or earned, but because of what God did and does. You are not loved for your potential or your perfection. You are loved because God made you, and you belong to God.

Unlike Shakespeare or van Gogh, who were as flawed and human as they were talented, our Artist doesn't close the manuscript and call it done. God's paintbrush is still in hand. We are being made new from our park prayer rocks and our practice rooms—not corrected using shame or some ideal we'll never reach but crafted by an Artist who wrote himself into our story and loved us with life.

We reach for our lenses for many reasons. We may need protection from an unhelpful or harmful view of God we inherited from our family or culture. We may need to hide from others and ourselves out of shame or fear of retribution. Maybe you realize that you've been worshiping or running from a God of your own making, one that fits neatly into your five-year plan or whose sole purpose is to find your faults. Maybe there's too much light pollution for you to believe the stars are even up there at all. Whatever it is, God sees you. God meets you there.

May you feel what it is to be seen through the eyes of an Artist. May you relish being a work of art yourself: beheld, beautiful, and beloved.

ARS NOVA

Let Art Shift Your Lens

One of art's greatest gifts is a new perspective. In this exercise, I'll ask you to consider your current lens or mindset and invite you to use art to find other ways of seeing your life.

1. Name a current circumstance you'd like to shift your mindset around. Try to be as neutral as possible. (e.g., I am unsure what to do next in my career.)
2. Now, name the current lens, a word or phrase that sums up how you see the circumstance. (e.g., stuck)
3. Find a work of art and take a moment to notice it. (Use the QR code at the back of this book to see some of van Gogh's *Olive Trees* or other works of music, sculpture, poetry, etc., which are used throughout this book.)

4. Choose one word that sums up the particular lens of this work of art. (e.g., colorful, majestic)
5. Return to your circumstance and look at it again through the lens you named for the work of art. Journal about what comes up. (e.g., In van Gogh's *Olive Trees*, he uses color sneakily; you don't even notice all the hues unless you look very closely. Maybe there is more than meets the eye with my career journey; maybe it isn't as simple as I want it to be, and I need to reflect more on how I feel, looking for the hidden "colors" that could perhaps light my way forward.)
6. Try the exercise again with a few different works of art. Write down anything important that comes up during these reflections. Share them with someone who will listen.

Chapter 2

Order the Chaos
Jan Vormann, Dispatchwork (2012)

> When God began to create the heavens and the earth, the earth was complete chaos, and darkness covered the face of the deep, while a wind from God swept over the face of the waters. Then God said, "Let there be light," and there was light. And God saw that the light was good, and God separated the light from the darkness. God called the light Day, and the darkness he called Night. And there was evening and there was morning, the first day.
>
> God saw everything that he had made, and indeed, it was very good.
>
> —Genesis 1:1–5, 31

How could it cost $45 to park here?

One day in Philadelphia, as I rushed toward the Kimmel Center, twenty-nine minutes before I was due on stage for a rehearsal, I found myself in a dilapidated, musty, low-ceilinged parking structure, bemoaning that almost half of that day's paycheck was about to go to parking my Toyota. I'd arrived too late to scour the surrounding neighborhoods for street parking, and I desperately needed to get inside for the downbeat.

As I exited the stairwell, trying to write the location of my car on the ephemeral whiteboard of my mom-brain, I caught a glimpse of myself in a shop window. My frizzy hair protruded sporadically from my snow hat, and I noticed that the music pocket of my backpack double case was open. After I frantically checked to make sure nothing had fallen out, I went to grab my lip balm from my purse, and dove hand-first into the waves of broken crayons and random junk my then-two-year-old daughter, Eva, had asked me to "hold." Rocks, sticks, trinkets, blocks, toys—they rolled everywhere, against a crinkly package of dried-out baby wipes. My thumb hit something sticky; I'd found the lip balm. I wiped the fuzz off the top and smeared it on my cracking lips. I sighed, threw everything back into my purse, and kept walking.

As I rounded a corner, the wind of winter made my eyes water. The salt had worked its magic to clear the sidewalks; the frozen water was separated from the dry land, but the snow looked as though it might topple onto my feet with the next gust. The gray afternoon light was slipping back into a darkness that seemed to cover the face of the deep all over again; it made everything seem dim and disheveled. It was a landscape that I fit right into, with my dark blue puffy coat and black boots. As I stopped to wait for the light, my eye was drawn to the side of a brick building at the corner, in the middle of which was a bright, colorful square.

Wait, were those . . . LEGOs?

I walked to the fence to get close. I felt the cold iron bars through the arms of my coat as I reached through to touch it. Someone had patched a large hole the size of an AC unit into the side of the brick with LEGO blocks. There was even a tiny toy window on the right side. The primary colors glowed in the dreary, wet evening. I paused for a moment and laughed out loud.

After rehearsal, down $45 and home in bed, I couldn't get the LEGO out of my mind. With a quick internet search, I learned about Dispatchwork, a community art project born in 2007, started by German artist Jan Vormann. I found a map of buildings across forty nations, each with a similar patch of bright yellows and blues, reds, whites, and oranges. Hundreds of individuals have joined around the globe, filling in the crevices, restoring facades, and mending cracks in their neighborhoods with toy blocks. It was chaotic, colorful, and childlike—all things I realized in that moment I was resisting.

Watery Chaos

The next day, forty-nine degrees and more storms in the forecast, somehow Eva convinced me to go for a walk. In the creation story of the Bible, scholars interpret the words that describe the raw material from which the world is created in various ways. The Hebrew word *tohu wa-bohu* is often translated as "formless void." Others refer to it as "watery chaos." The latter felt very on brand for winter in the mid-Atlantic, to be honest. The salt and slush, mud pools perched to become ice again; it's like regular chaos, only wet.

As Eva jumped from one brown, formless void to the next, as I tried to keep her from falling over snow drifts and into traffic, as I ruminated on my rehearsal the night before, one word kept bouncing around in my brain: *chaos*.

It was a full season of many good things—new opportunities as a freelance musician and professor, the bright light of a child who suddenly wanted to explore everything and be everywhere, and the thaw from winter seemed imminent. Yet, between all the ears being infected, the toys always underfoot, the strategically placed snow days, the attempt to balance a multi-passionate creative life—well, I felt a lot like a car on black ice: *Just* when I thought I had a rhythm, I'd start skidding again. The daily allotment of sunlight was meager, and the watery chaos was making for a grouchy mama and an antsy Eva. I found myself holding my breath at the state of the world, waiting for something to be different, lacking the energy or the willpower to attempt to make it so. I looked down and noticed Eva was shivering and soaked. I led her back to the house to change.

The hardest thing about rejecting the whole "new-year, new-you" propaganda every January is that I *do* long to feel new. Don't you? It is so tempting to fall into the trap of getting a gym membership, buying a planner, or starting a diet because you're waist-deep in a life that just isn't quite working. There have been moments in life when it felt more painful to stay the same than it was to change. As a coach, I've heard clients say something similar. "I'm sick and tired of feeling sick and tired." And so, we pull not-so-gently at the loose threads of all that armor we are wearing with what some call "black trash bag energy," which is less "new-year, new-you" and more Extreme Makeover Life Edition. "Is this where it hurts? Here? What about here?" Until the whole thing begins to fall away, and we stand there exposed. Despite the cold, it's a relief to let go, to let ourselves change.

But this year, even if I purged my house or organized my purse, I had a feeling that something would still feel wrong. I knew the true issue was deeper. That one kitchen drawer ends up being the drop zone, no matter what we do. Parking costs $45. House projects are started and abandoned. The calendar, graciously (and suspiciously) empty one minute, then overflowing with drop-offs and pick-ups and grocery orders, and work trips the next minute. I loved our life, but sometimes it felt like a Jackson Pollock painting. The problem wasn't the stuff; it was the chaos.

As I threw Eva's wet clothes into the washing machine, I felt defeated and broken. *If God is my Artist, and I am God's creation, then why was I such a mess?*

Where the Art Is

A week or so later, during *yet another* snow day, while I needed to be working, I decided to do an art project with my Eva.

(Truth: I was working on my computer at the table while she was playing with our copious amounts of art supplies.) If she was a cartoon, she'd have been surrounded by a cloud of glitter, construction paper, glue, and washable paint. She was having fun and making an industrial-strength mess. Exhausted, thinking of how I would have to clean glitter out of the grout, I jumped in and tried to contain it.

"Mama, don't," she said, "Art is messy."

That's when I realized it.

We can't be creative without chaos. Why did this truth surprise me? Chaos is the raw material of life. Chaos is where the art is.

I was frustrated and tired because I was trying to eradicate the chaos, make my life as neat as a correctly folded fitted sheet, when I knew deep down, I was powerless to stop it. And thanks to Eva, I suddenly understood this was good news. Instead of the guilt and shame of having a chaotic home or life, I wanted to work to see the *hope* in it. Like the creative energy of Genesis, as someone bearing the image of God, I am empowered to bring order to the chaos in whatever ways my limited human hands can. I longed to take a cue from the Creator of the Universe and call it good.

I've spent a great deal of time in my life, before and after becoming a mother, attempting to make my life less chaotic. In school, I'd practice my scales every morning before dawn; I'd plan out my schedule down to the half hour. When I was pregnant with Eva, I bought stickers for the dozens of tiny baby hangers and organized her closet of hand-me-downs into neat sections labeled newborn, three-month, six-month, and twelve-month. And yet, every time, no matter what, somewhere along the way, the schedule fell apart, and the closet became a mess of stained onesies and rogue socks. I still don't see a weekend commitment coming. I fail to remember to buy milk. I'm too tired to tidy up or load the dishwasher. We plan the meals, and no one wants to eat chicken tonight, including me.

I want to feel prepared, to anticipate the needs of those around me, stretch into the white space of free time. I want to be one of those people who always does the laundry on Saturdays or plans the meals for the entire week on Sundays, and yet I keep "failing." I fail for many reasons, but the central one is that life is chaotic, especially in this season.

Instead of trying to change that, since that winter day in the cartoon cloud of craft mess with Eva, when my two-year-old delivered a message straight from my Creator, I am learning to embrace the chaos, to take a cue from my daughter, to enjoy the practice of ordering it, and call it good.

Ordering the chaos means seeing the disorganized circus that is my life as an invitation to accept, rather than a problem to solve. When we judge the mess, we can miss the art that is asking to be born in it. We forget to look around and notice the people in the clouds of glitter with us; we're so busy judging ourselves and—let's be honest—others, that we fail to creatively say yes to the opportunity that chaos provides: to be together, to problem solve, to love one another and our life, to be surprised by joy.

Using LEGO blocks to mend a crumbling facade is one of my favorite examples of ordering the chaos. Those blocks that day, too, were a divine wind across the surface of the deep, inviting me to remember my *tohu wa-bohu*–ness, to stop judging myself, and let God call it good.

What if we met the challenges we face with the most unexpected and playful answers, rather than following our first instincts to tear down the structure, crash diet, and start over, but instead mend what we can, when we can, with what we have?

The deeper lesson is this: Sometimes, in an effort to find order, we need to make an even bigger mess. We must remove everything from that one cabinet and let its contents air out on the countertop. We must take stock of all that we have so we can know how to use it. Then, I could believe that in my biggest personal messes, in all that is chaotic and even broken in me, God is working. Our Creator's first action in the beginning was to breathe over the watery chaos and bring order. What if God is still doing that today, calling us to do the same? We are made in the image of God, the Creator, after all.

Ordering the chaos means putting aside what we don't need and bringing order to what we do. It is buying ingredients to make a meal without knowing exactly when or how we will eat it. It is working to get there early enough to find street parking, improvising when we don't. All the while trusting that God has color and joy to show us along the way. Mostly, it's about not feeling bad when the pesky pandemonium of life appears again like a wet dog at the back door. It's remembering that creating a life is an art, and art is messy. When there's chaos, the very energy of creation stands before us, brimming with possibility.

Wild-Goose Chase

In Celtic spirituality, the Spirit is often depicted as a wild gray-lag goose.

Unlike the calm, gentle, elegant dove of the Bible, the goose is known for its honking call, unpredictable nature, and aggression, especially when defending its territory. This Celtic spiritual tradition epitomizes the Holy Goose's disruptive and transformational disposition: powerful, wild, and untamed. In a word: chaotic.

Inside those moments of life, when it feels like one long, wild-goose chase, trying to find the cap to your lip balm in the bottom of a Mary Poppins bag, what if you could trust that what you're chasing (or what's chasing you?) is wise and loving beyond your understanding? What if the chaos invites us to trust in God, who is still sovereign over creation, who knows how to rest?

When we create, we are connected to something larger than ourselves. This means that we can believe that there is more at play than we can see in each moment, we can open our hands and make room for surprise and delight. We can stop resisting the chaos and start seeing the Spirit of love and creative power in it, fiercely defending us with a loud, chaotic honk.

We cannot let our desire for order, certainty, and predictability steal our joy; the creation narrative invites us into another story. The chaos and the unexpected detours are ripe with creative possibility, an invitation for you to keep saying yes despite the mess.

Ordering chaos invites us to remember what my husband Edwin always says when I find myself attempting to eradicate it once again: "We are not problems to be solved but people to be loved."

I hope you will join me, as you face your own chaos, to improvise with what you have, to embrace the Jackson Pollock–ness of life, to patch the side of your crumbling facade with LEGO. I hope you'll come face to face with your human limits and find there the incredibly messy, raw material of God's creative love. I hope you will laugh at your life, especially when it is at its most chaotic, that you will never begrudge yourself the wild-goose chase.

Here's to finding cheap parking and the cap to the lip balm, the breath of God's closeness right there in the chaotic joy of each and every day, to call it good . . . or, at least, good enough.

ARS NOVA

Let Art Be Messy

1. Pick a work of art that you know rather well. It can be a work of visual art, a piece of music, a novel or play, or anything in between.
2. Reverse-deconstruct in your head the elements that the artist has organized. Write them down in an informal

list. This is not an academic assignment; let it be chaotic and fun.

For example, Shakespeare took a complex plot with a large number of characters, the story of the King of Denmark and his family, and used the twenty-six letters of the English alphabet to tell a story of corruption, revenge, mortality, politics, family, loyalty, and love (to name a few). He used monologue, soliloquy, scene, a play-within-a-play, wordplay, puns, a fight scene, irony, asides, a skull and other props, costumes, scenery, etc., etc., etc.

3. Close your eyes and imagine the elements of this work of art (the words you wrote) in a disorganized pile.
4. Now, take a deep breath, wave your hand gently through the air, and imagine the pieces moving into place, the chaos ordered.
5. Reflect: Looking at the chaos of your life, ask yourself: what creative potential is here now?

Interlude

Flowering Onion

My life has become so colorful since I started working with blocked artists. So have my walls.

Your package arrives as a thank-you gift, and I am the thankful one.

You are a Flutist (or Flautist?) I don't know how you choose to spell it, but either way, I know in your mind it is capitalized and always follows your name.

The note that accompanies the small package says that some people call these flowers you've painted "purple sensations," and your rendering in oil lives up to the name. I know this one—it is a flowering onion. The impossibly skinny stalk erupts unapologetically into a spikey, prickly ball, and the plant's joy fills the small square frame you've meticulously covered in bubble wrap for the journey from your house to mine.

They don't value oil painting as a skill set at the music conservatory, and you believe them when they say your painting practice is a beautiful waste of time.

Holding your creation in my weary hands, chapped from winter's wind, I consider the bulbs waiting underground. I wonder if you know the difference between a flowering onion and a culinary one.

The color and life bounce from the canvas just like your flute's staccato. Your voice, across art forms, sings.

Will you allow yourself to fill your life's frame?

The strong and sturdy, flowering firework can be planted late into the fall; it is impervious to ravenous deer. But inside the same plant is a hefty-husked promise of sharp intensity and tearful pungency, the earthy sweetness that fills the house. These creations both exist inside one papery bulb.

What if our Creator never intended us to be only one thing?

The difference between the onions is a question of cultivation, patience, grace.

These are the shades of color, the gifts, I most long to give you.

Chapter 3

Listening Is the Work
Johannes Brahms, Symphony No. 4, Finale (1885)

God spoke today in flowers,
And I, who was waiting on words,
almost missed the conversation.

—Ingrid Goff-Maidoff

If Brahms lived like us, in the days of internet browsers and word processors, he would have had the tab for his Symphony No. 1 open for twenty-two years. From early sketches to the work's premiere, Brahms worked on one fifty-minute piece of music for a whole third of his life.

He suffered from what music historians call the "anxiety of influence," which for Brahms meant constantly listening behind him for the metaphorical footsteps of the symphonic giant, Beethoven. Early in his career, Robert Schumann, fellow composer and music critic, anointed Brahms as the Next Great Classical Innovator. After Franz Joseph Haydn, Mozart, and Beethoven, Brahms would be the one to write the next great symphony. Beethoven's 10th. *No pressure, Johannes.*

I imagine him at his piano with his round, bearded face in his hands, candlelight flickering, ashes from the pages he'd abandoned to the flames still floating in the air. He infamously set his music on fire before anyone could see it, destroying drafts and entire leather-bound scores. The manuscript of the first movement of the symphony is marked as "lost": lost to the blaze of creative U-turns, the all-consuming conflagration of his fear, perfectionism, doubt, and perhaps a little vanity.

Mind the Gap

There is a time in every artist's life when we become aware of what Ira Glass calls "the Gap." The space between our taste—the vision of the thing we are making, the hope of what it could be—and the (often depressing) reality of what it is today. We get into creative work because we see this vision, we hear its call. And by some miracle, at the most random times, when we are reading a novel or loading the dishwasher, the light flashes, and all we can do is stand still and listen. We hear the sounds we want to make in our head; we know the feelings we want the story to evoke or how the finished painting should look. And we know when the work we are making isn't cutting it.

It isn't that we are always too hard on ourselves (although sometimes we are). It's more that we've heard a melody we cannot unhear—a flicker, a thread—resonant with some inner longing, and we hold on to it so desperately through the cacophony of life, willing it into being. We labor in service to something as nebulous as a feeling we had once while we were walking the dog. And even just a moment later, when it was once so bright and clear, the sound of that spiritual song becomes faint. We get stuck in the echo chamber of self-consciousness, hearing nothing but the recurring clangor of our own thoughts. Some days, that gap feels like an impenetrable ravine between us and completion. The many imperfections of the work taunt from down below; it's too terrifying to step to the edge.

In short, I get why Brahms turned an early symphony draft into a piano concerto mid-stream. I get why he set his scores on fire.

Don't Set Your Computer on Fire

Recently, my creative process has felt like walking into a familiar room, only blindfolded. I sit down to a blinking cursor on a big project. One that will take me years to finish, something I feel, in some ways, I have been working on (and longing to complete) all my life. It is finally time to make this thing, and amazingly, it is now my job to tend this seed and shepherd the work into the world. Cue fireworks and celebration emojis.

And yet, as I get down to work, I can't help but think of Brahms. While I don't hear Beethoven's footsteps behind me, I do sense a deeply judgmental inner mean girl waiting for my greatest fears to be confirmed. My original idea cowers in the corner like a small, scared animal, and I fight the overwhelming impulse to crumple the metaphorical paper and throw it into the actual fire.

Created Things Speak

Last time I stared down a large-scale creative project, I had the time and made the space every week to listen to what it wanted to be. I gave myself a weekly deadline, and the making felt less like creating something out of nothing and more like getting out of the way. But that process wasn't working this time. After weeks of wringing my hands and staring anxiously at the blank canvas, this was the message I received loud and clear: This one will not come through the same old channels.

Lest we forget, creative projects speak. In a desire to name the document or feel productive or keep the death grip tight on what little control we think we have, we do not—I do not—always listen. In lieu of walking to the periphery of my abilities and standing along the edge of that abyss, I get busy, manic. The answers never come through more striving, yet still I strive.

The Sum of the Parts

I knew an oboe teacher once who used to say to his students, "Don't take 'no' for an answer from an inanimate object." With sheer will, hard work, dedication, and more and more sacrifice, he implied, you (a living, breathing human being) can make the oboe and your reeds (inanimate objects) do what you want them to do. You are the one with the brain, so make those dead things work.

I can see what he was getting at, but now, years later, I think these sentiments put me at odds with my intuition and the spiritual invitation of art-making. It is deep work, listening to the materials in your hands. While they aren't "living" in an earthly sense, when the cane becomes a reed, or the words become a poem, they are brought to a kind of life, which sometimes has a will of its own. Even a pottery novice can feel the energy from a mound of clay.

I'm not sure who else could do that—could perform such alchemy—besides some deeper reality, besides God. Dry bones live. Lines leap like a ballerina off the page. God can speak through everyday "inanimate" objects, can use these humble materials to call every artist to some deeper purpose.

Bossing the materials around might work for a while, but it puts striving in the seat of the ultimate Way-Maker.

At some point in the process, each new project makes it clear: My usual try-hard, perfectionist mindset, creating from a place of striving—she has no power here. This is not something I can bend to my will by sheer force. Instead, it requires a profound and uneasy stillness of soul. It calls me into murky, opaque waters, where I surrender my complete attention.

I stand there, teetering on the edge, arms up, ready to fight.

If creativity is a spiritual practice, if art is an open door to something beyond us, then why does it sometimes feel so much like a battlefield?

A Different Kind of Battle Cry

In my faith tradition, we are prone to embroidering certain Bible verses onto throw pillows or creating cute little placards above the kitchen window. Perhaps one of the most common ones is Psalm 46:10: "Be still and know that I am God." All my life, I have heard this Scripture evoked as a mantra for rest and other fuzzy feelings.

And yet, as I am often slow to do with verses I memorized as a child, when you look at the context of this ancient Hebrew song, we see that the writer of this psalm confronts his own crisis of confidence while actual battles rage around him.

> *Therefore we will not fear, though the earth should change,*
> *though the mountains shake in the heart of the sea,*
> *though its waters roar and foam,*
> *though the mountains tremble with its tumult.*
> *(Psalm 46:10, vv. 2–3)*

The psalmist pauses amid the raging battle, the nations in uproar, and hears God speak above the tumult. Interestingly, God doesn't say, over the cries of terror and destruction, "Work harder! Don't take 'no' for an answer! Keep striving!" In that moment, Ultimate Reality commands, "Be still and know that I am God."

Later in the chapter, the psalmist points out that at a single utterance of God's voice, the earth melts or softens. Put down your sword—or for the artist—set down the brush, lift your hands from the keyboard. Be still and know.

Don't just toss these words on a loveseat. Put them on a sticky note at your writing desk. Paint them large on a placard in your studio. God is commanding us, in the face of the inner and outer wars that we fight, to get very still and listen; let God's voice soften you.

What Brahms Heard

It reached the point when the only thing standing between Brahms and the finish line for his first symphony was a melody for the finale. He was living in Switzerland at the time.

I imagine him showing up to the piano where he composed with a soul-deep weariness. I see him removing his spectacles and rubbing his eyes, glancing over at the unfinished song-cycle that was likely coming more easily than this God-forsaken symphony. I see him taking a long exhale, putting his quill down, and walking out the front door.

God spoke that day through, of all things, the alphorn (a Swiss folk instrument). In a letter he penned on September 12, 1868, to his dear friend Clara Schumann (a famous pianist and wife of Robert Schumann), he scribbled down a melody he heard on that walk. From across the valley, a voice echoed: a hauntingly heroic and beautiful melody, the key that unlocked his symphony.

The Sound of Stillness

Amid the battle cries of your artist life, stillness might feel impossible. Maybe it sounds like one more task to check off your to-do list. That would be missing the point. The way of creative joy is not paved with more striving but less. The Hebrew word for "be still" in Psalm 46 is translated as "loosen" or "release" elsewhere in Scripture. One translation says,

Step out of the traffic! Take a long,
loving look at me, your High God,
above politics, above everything. (Psalm 46:10, The Message)

The command "be still and know that I am God" is not a pretty platitude—or a self-absorbed command you must strive in your own strength to follow—but a booming voice across the battlefield, inviting you to receive the grace that is already yours. And the good news is that it is as simple as taking a walk in the woods, of taking a long, loving look at all God has already done in your life. It is a posture of trust, of deep listening, loosened and open to whatever gifts are waiting just across the Alpine Valley.

Write This

As Ingrid Gott-Maidoff says, sometimes God speaks in flowers, and when we expect words, we might risk missing the entire conversation. At the crack of 5 a.m., when my alarm goes off again, rousing me for my daily writing time—I hit snooze, as I often do. *What's the point of sitting at my computer if I have nothing to say?* That's when I heard it. The dawn's chorus of birds in the tree outside my window were alive and God wanted me to know. I lay there and listened like Brahms to an alphorn. What was God saying through the robin's song, the spring morning?

This. Write this.

Birds sing in the mornings during spring for all the reasons you would guess—defending their nests, signaling danger—but they also sing to be known to their future mates and neighbors. Scientists believe that each bird has a unique song, like a signature.

Creating, then—sitting down, even when you fear you have nothing to offer—is like a piercing bird call in a dark morning, a persistent and faithful sign of life, a celebration of making it through the night, a chance to find your own unique song.

What the robins by my bedroom window taught me that morning, what God is still teaching me, is that listening is the work.

Listen Up

If God is an artist, then there are melodies and words and colors waiting in the stillness, divine gifts. They are breadcrumbs leading the way out and through the battles we wage, usually of our own making and self-sabotaging.

We are not alone inside our creative efforts, in traversing the Gap. God, a fellow artist, goes with us and closes that distance.

Whether it takes you twenty-two years or twenty-two minutes to bring the thing you are making into the world, what would it shift for you to believe that the materials you work with are alive with God's goodness and grace? That they speak of what should come next, who they are for, and how they will be born?

The act of paying attention, being still long enough to stop the incessant striving in your own strength—this type of listening is essential to life as an artist. Listening is the work. Inherent in each moment is an invitation to trust something already at work, to walk out of the studio and into the forest, to let the art speak.

Will you listen?

ARS NOVA

Audio Divina "Divine Listening"

Originating with the Desert Mothers and Fathers in the third or fourth centuries, *Lectio Divina* (Divine Reading) is a practice that helps you read Scripture more prayerfully. *Audio Divina* is a kind of deep listening as a form of prayer. While this would mean listening to sacred music intended for worship settings, I invite us to a more expansive repertoire, from birdsong to ballad.

1. *Audio* (Listen): Choose a portion of a piece of music from the book's playlist (via the QR code found in the back of the book) or turn to whatever music you enjoy. (You might try the music I mentioned in this chapter, Brahms's Symphony No. 1, *finale*, and specifically the alphorn solo he heard while walking. It usually begins in the last fifteen to twenty minutes of most recordings.) Regardless of what you choose, reduce distractions and listen deeply.
2. *Meditatio* (Meditate): Listen to the same section again. If you aren't sure what to listen for or what you're hearing, check out the list below, where I offer you examples of musical elements that musicians and composers use to make music expressive. Choose one from that list to listen for, or let whatever element you're meant to hear jump out at you as you listen a second time.
3. *Oratio* (Pray): Turn now to an inward listening. Ask what you are meant to hear from this listening session. Make sure to leave silence to receive whatever answers may come.
4. *Contemplatio* (Contemplate): Receive what is yours to take away. Sit not in action but in complete trust. Find a posture of rest before finishing this session.

Musical Elements to Listen For

- Lyrics: the words sung. What word or phrases stick out to you?
- Pulse: the speed of the beat of a piece of music.
- Pitch: how high or low the notes are. Notice if they are moving up or down or staying the same.
- Timbre: the tone quality of an instrument or piece of music in general. What images does the timbre evoke?
- Rhythm: how fast or slow the notes are moving against the pulse.
- Others: tonality, texture, melody, harmony, form, dynamics, intervals, instrumentation, etc.

Chapter 4

Hang On to the Thread
Antoni Gaudí, Basílica de la Sagrada Família (Started 1882)

> Then suddenly a woman who had been suffering from a flow of blood for twelve years came up behind him and touched the fringe of his cloak, for she was saying to herself, "If I only touch his cloak, I will be made well." Jesus turned, and seeing her he said, "Take heart, daughter; your faith has made you well." And the woman was made well from that moment.
>
> —Matthew 9:20–22

There is a baby grand piano, of all things, at the airport gate. I am balancing my café au lait on my leg and passing out breakfast pastries to all the hungry people in my care when I hear—across the hordes of people in duty-free, through the glass gateways holding back all of us who are hurrying up to wait, around the corner and way down at the end of the terminal—Scott Joplin's "Maple Leaf Rag" rise above the noise.

As a professional musician, you'd think the sight of a beautiful instrument, free for anyone to sit down and play, would be a joyful one, a welcoming, exciting, delightful invitation to create in the cracks. I'm ashamed to say that, in truth, when I see pianos in public with a sign that says, "PLAY ME," my first reaction is dread. Many of my coaching clients and musician friends say the same. As the designated “music person” (even though I’m an oboist and not a pianist, mind you), I fear that my friends and fellow travelers will look at me and say, “Play something!”

What do I even have memorized?
Is it flashy or beautiful or good enough?
What if people start making requests?

I usually crawl into myself, perhaps politely decline, and then feel bad about it later.

But this time, as my children started dancing wildly to ragtime, making crumbs fly everywhere, I let the music wash over me. It is a young college student playing. I studied him. His eyes were focused but bright. I tapped my foot, too. I accepted the new lightness in the somber air, the syncopated lilt of this unapologetically joyful music that falls over us like the powdered sugar on my children’s abandoned croissants.

Before we boarded the plane, my family and I ordered the chaos (i.e., the pastry debris) we’d left behind in the terminal.

“Thanks for playing,” I tell him when we pass each other in line a few moments later.

“You’re welcome,” he says, glowingly, “Happy New Year.”

Later on the plane, I chat with my husband about how much joy the piano brought me.

He listens, smiling in that knowing way of his, and then asks me, “What is God teaching you?”

Word Search

Each December/January I pick a word for the year ahead, to guide and inspire me toward the growth I hope to see in myself. This year, several options tumble around in my brain like clothes in a drier, but I can’t seem to find the words I want to live by. I have many intentions (I don't dare call them resolutions), but I am attempting these slowly and loosely, with expectations set to "January in Michigan" temperature settings: lower than low.

As someone who writes about personal development and who historically loves to plan and dream of the future, I'm surprised at the murkiness I feel around my word of the year this go-round. I'm intrigued by my disinterest in thinking beyond this week.

I know from reading about such things that hyper-focusing on the present can be a trauma response. Maybe that's too strong a word for my situation—there is no "capital *T* Trauma" that is affecting me right now—but I am horrified daily by all the suffering around me. Yesterday, I drove by what I now know was a doubly fatal car accident. A close friend of mine is going through a messy relationship breakdown. People I know have lost everything in the wildfires in California. Loss, loss, loss.

I have arrived here at the beginning of another year, grateful to be alive and safe, yet considering a long-term hibernation until there's more daylight and the news is marginally better. A word of the year feels like a sledgehammer when the tool I need is a pillow.

This wouldn't be such a problem if I weren't staring down a deadline—a project that is so important to me, not only because multiple people are expecting me to finish, but because it is a work of art I feel I was born to create.

Lately, I have become a petty, whiny child every time I try to push the "discipline button" and open the work. Then I feel bad for feeling bad. Am I not grateful for the chance to do this? Why don't I buck up and get over myself and just do it? I need a word of the year to help me arrive at my desk ready to listen. I need a word of the year that feels gentle enough to meet me in this fragile, foggy, freezing moment and strong enough to shake me from this slumber into action and, if not thrust into creative flow, provide at least a slow drip of some kind of motivation.

What word is that?

Hold On

Over Christmas break, we traveled to Europe for the first time as a family of five, with La Mami (The Mom), my mother-in-law, who also came along. It was an unforgettable adventure, gallivanting with twenty-six roller bags, fifteen pounds of snacks, and one monstrosity of a double stroller through France and Spain with two children under seven. (The adults outnumbered the kids at least!) While there were small meltdowns (from the kids and me both) and while I did come home needing pain management for my teeth grinding, overall it was a lovely trip.

Back home, both kids mercifully at school for the first time in three weeks, my husband and I were reflecting on the trip and, in particular, how much we learned about our children—their rhythms, their hilarious facial expressions (mostly Eli), and their uniquely weird and wonderful way of moving through the world. By the light of the Eiffel Tower, by the rainbow rays of stained glass in La Sagrada Família, my little family looked different to me all of a sudden.

I'm struck by how being in close proximity to each other without interruption or break—the *quantity* time, which is more elusive at home—impacted our intimacy and deepened our connection so quickly. All the parenting books tell you how important *quality* time is over quantity—limit screen time and make the most of the evenings after school because, with work and life, those brief hours and eighteen summers are all you get. I don't disagree that we should make the most of that time, but I don't like the scarcity mindset behind that reasoning at all. Mama needs a break sometimes! But as exhausting and stressful as having my kids within arm's reach for three weeks straight was, I can see how the sheer quantity of shared experience creates deep connection and lasting memories.

Just being together, even in the generally low-quality moments—like transatlantic flights where we all sat in front of screens for hours—has shifted something within me. The inside jokes and new rituals, my deepening skill of anticipating needs, felt like growth as a mother; I felt myself loving them more and better.

One new thing we learned was how to stay together in a crowd. When we are without the stroller, walking in a congested airport or a busy parking lot, Eli loves to hold my hand, but Eva, my almost-seven-year-old, does not so much. I'm terrified of us getting separated, so Eva and I compromise. "Hold on to my sweater!" I yell in the crowded airport train in Paris, and as we push through the masses of travelers and roller bags, I can feel the gentle pull of her little hand against my back. I know she's with me. This is just one routine, one small, familiar intimacy that we developed over those three weeks. But it's stuck with me in the way that trivial things do when they have something to teach.

We are carrying so much into each and every new year: grief mixed with cautious optimism, big and small fears for our and other people's children, confused and angry prayers. We hold on to hope like a child at their mother's back, battered by the onslaught of hardship and suffering. We hold on, and when we finally break through the thick crowd of overthinking and bone-deep exhaustion, we find that somehow, against all odds, we have not let go.

Then it occurs to me, this is how I will write this book. I'll hold on to the hem of its garment and keep walking. I'll grab on to the thread of that idea that I have carried with me all my life, a gift that I believe didn't come from me, and follow it back to the one who does not let me go, who brings healing.

For me, this looks like showing up to write even when I don't know what to say. It means choosing to trust that there is wisdom and love guiding me if I am willing to keep going. Hanging on to the thread becomes a filter through which I run every decision. As I choose what music or audiobook to listen to on my commute, I ask myself, will this help me hang on, will it deepen my connection to this dream, this calling, this faith, or not? I will hone my inner knowing; I will bring new attention to my mind and my body; I will practice, even when it is hard.

For Dear Life

Though the exact source of the phrase is unknown, Franklin D. Roosevelt is often quoted as saying, "When you come to the end of your rope, tie a knot and hang on." I can see a nineties motivational poster with a small yellow kitten clinging to a knotted cord in my mind's eye. I don't know about you, but more this year than others, I feel remarkably like that scaredy-cat from that photo, hanging on by a thread.

But what if we could recast this "hanging on" mantra into something more empowering? Maybe the piano in the terminal is teaching me that there are many threads, many ropes, to tie a knot in and grab on to, to lead us home. It is teaching me that art and inspiration are everywhere, and while it can feel like the world—the pace and unpredictability of our lives—is dead-set on separating us from the creative flow, from the ah-ha moments, from God's joy, it's still there, waiting, just out of sight.

When we feel like we use all our energy to keep pushing against the crowd, holding back the weight of despair that threatens to trample us, when we are tempted to let the cynicism or the busyness pry loose our grip and make us let go, what if hanging on by a thread is not a call for help but a way home, a way through?

Maybe you aren't ready or able to hold hands with creative joy, with that dream you are chasing, but could you grab the back of your Maker's sweater? Do you trust God enough to lead you? Will you foster that connection through *quantity* time, the rugged and imperfect and sacred practice of showing up, weary and wanting? When you find yourself awake at 2 a.m. due to jetlag or when you're too tired/busy/sad/anxious to create, will you do what you can to care for yourself, to provide that endless supply of snacks that travelers seem to need, and not disown your own inner knowing, God's call on your life, for some guru or mentor?

Will you join me in hanging on for dear life to the thread of who you feel called to become, to trust that God holds you?

What if creativity and making things we care about, from a meal to a manuscript, is less about being brilliant and coming up with a way forward and more about a dogged, stubborn, persistent, sweaty-palmed reaching out, hanging on?

If I have learned anything from that magical (read: exhausting) New Year's trip to Europe with my family, it's that being together, yes, in the grand castles and awe-inspiring cathedrals, but also in unclean airport bathrooms and ice-laden sidewalks, dancing together with equal abandon under shimmering landmarks and fluorescent lights of a depressing terminal—it is hanging on to one another, hanging on to joy, choosing each day to show up is how we keep going, how we find our way.

The Threads Hang On to Us

Construction of the Basílica de la Sagrada Família (The Church of the Holy Family) began in Barcelona under the direction of architect Francisco de Paula del Villar in March 1882. Villar resigned the next year, and the young Antoni Gaudí assumed responsibility for the design. Gaudí took the project in a remarkable direction.

What is so exceptional about this structure to me, a lover of all things modern, besides the church's massive towers and exquisite stained glass, is the way it merges the Gothic style with Art Nouveau, the old and the new slamming right into one another, forever altering the skyline of Barcelona. You come around the corner, and your eyes are drawn up; the otherworldly structure steals your breath. The giant cranes and teetering scaffolding are the only clues that this work of art remains unfinished.

Forty years into the project, Gaudí was hit by a tram and died tragically in 1926. The cathedral, which he had spent over half his life working on, was only about 15 percent complete. Spain broke into civil war, and construction was delayed. Many of the original models of La Sagrada Família burned in fires. New architects were hired. Work continued off and on, delayed again and again in our day by both permit and pandemic. The estimated completion date of the main structural work is now tentatively set for 2026. That's right: 100 years after the architect's death, 141 years after the first stone was laid. Soon(ish), La Sagrada Família will be done, and when complete, it will stand as the tallest church in the world.

As my neck began to hurt from staring up at the Passion Facade, an epoch of stone storytelling, I wanted to ask you: How will you hang on to the thread of your creative dreams when the inevitable interruptions arise? How will you build and rebuild, keep going, despite everything?

In that moment, I noticed one of the disciples on the stone structure looked a lot like the pictures of Gaudí from the museum, with his furrowed brow and square face. Later, I read that some sources claim the sculptor who took over the design did this as a subtle homage to the man who conceived the building.

Remembering the cathedral now, back home in Michigan, I see Gaudí in it everywhere. At one point, he'd built himself a home inside, moved into the temple workshop. Today, he is buried in the crypt down below the altar. Every stone and symbol of the place hums with his eccentric, devout, passionate, and joyful spirit. He reminds me that not only do we hang on to the threads of our creative callings, but by some miracle, our threads hang on to us.

Tie a Knot

Maybe you can't inhabit your dreams just yet. Maybe we'll never be the mastermind behind a UNESCO World Heritage Site. Maybe you aren't even sure what is on the other end of that thread you're hanging on to. Maybe all you can muster is sitting in the studio for five minutes a few times a week.

Here's to seeing: That is not nothing.

Here's to normalizing the long game, because let's be honest, even if Gaudí had lived longer, he would not have seen the cathedral finished in his lifetime.

Here's to taking a cue from a fearless Catalan whose unwavering vision sings to me through time.

Here's to letting yourself enjoy the pianos you find on your path, to no longer waiting for the products of our work to be finished before we celebrate, to no longer believing that it is all or nothing.

The bleeding woman from Matthew's gospel, who reaches out for the hem of Jesus's cloak, reminds me of the desperate acts of faith required in art-making. Her faith made her well, Jesus said, but why? Because she was willing to reach out in hope, and through that God-given audacity and courage, she was healed. Like a child in a crowded train who grabs her mother's sweater, we can know that reaching out for a single thread of creative inspiration, these gifts from the divine, it is the hanging on that leads to profound transformation.

Here's to holding on fiercely to the thread of our creative calling, letting it lead us to something greater than we can imagine—a healing that includes us but is much bigger, more resonant, more expansive than we even know.

As the missteps and mistakes threaten to steal our joy, as the wars rage and calamities fall like locusts, we will keep turning our attention back to the creative song and let that "still small voice" keep inching us forward into the unknown (1 Kings 19:11–13 KJV).

We will trust that at the other end of that rope is our Creator, the Architect of history, who loves us, who delights in tenacious acts of desperate faith. Grabbing the hem of the Maker's garment, feeling hope's gentle tug, means more than productivity or focus; it brings wholeness.

Remember the last time you felt like writing? Remember when the poem bubbled up in you out of nowhere? The flicker of a spark of how to fix the painting or the way the music could go, appearing like some distant unfinished tower in the imagined skyline of your psyche?

Remember that feeling? Now, tie a knot and hang on.

ARS NOVA

Let Art Be a Thread

If we imagine each created thing as a thread leading us back to its creator and the creator's creator, and the creator's creator's creator and so on, using art as a spiritual gateway means intentionally choosing art whose thread leads us back to somewhere we'd like to go. Bringing awareness to how art makes us feel is a great place to start.

Bring a favorite work of art to mind and reflect on its spiritual power and specific threads of meaning.

1. What does this work of art do to me physically?
   Examples: Tears to my eyes, breathe more deeply, sit on the edge of my seat, sway in rhythm, or tap my foot

2. What does it remind me of?
   Examples: Childhood, a loved one, a trip I took
3. What "threads" does this work of art help me hang on to?
   Examples: Faith in a loving Creator, dreams of creating a similar work of art, fighting for our planet
4. Reflect on what you've written and look for actionable steps, opportunities to reach out and grab on to the threads that resonate for you.

Part II

Shadow

The Pencil

> In suffering lies the song of poetry, like a hymn that liberates and penetrates to the bottom of the truth.
>
> —Flaben Lacombe (1921–1993), French journalist and poet, prisoner at Dachau, 1944–1945

To create in the camps was punishable by death.
One poem, scribbled hurriedly
with a pencil stolen from the foreman
kept a man called Mirco Camia alive.

I walk the grounds of Dachau, 80 years since
and hear the scratch of the granite against the book of death.
The men who stripped them of dignity and clothing
added arrivals with that pencil:
it turned mother, brother, child,
from name to number,
a pencil for erasing the dead,
who cannot be erased.

Mirco found words of a cell block friend,
a belonging to one who owned nothing.
The stanzas, a song sung silently for decades.
Daily, the poem unlocked an inner gate,
penetrated to the bottom of a truth:
Art is how God loves us.
But art is also how we love,
how we go on,
how we practice personhood.

What if each act of creation is still a potent word carved
into the wooden side of a bunker?
A mercy, an ember, to tend in the night,
to sustain in the shadows?

What if each Star of David
scratched into the underside of a metal bowl,
made with dangerous hope and courageous defiance,
is an altar?

They created with what they had,
because creating was all they had.
But where was their Creator?

If a poem could save a life,
then maybe all of art
is a rescue mission,
a flair in an inky-black sky.

What if words could split open barbed wire,
shield you in the death strip?

May you dare to believe that the Creator
of words and worlds,
knows you by name
that your Maker never once looked away
that you are listed there
in the Book of Life.

I pray we are ever brave enough
to steal the pencil.

Chapter 5

Shadow Careers and Simple Gifts
Joseph Brackett, "Simple Gifts" (1848)

'Tis the gift to be simple, 'tis the gift to be free,
'Tis the gift to come down where I ought to be;
And when we find ourselves in the place just right,
'Twill be in the valley of love and delight.
When true simplicity is gained,
To bow and to bend we shan't be ashamed;
to turn, turn, will be my delight.
Till by turning, turning we come round right.

—Text to "Simple Gifts" a Shaker dance

Professor J heaved the volumes onto the sturdy tables of the stuffy, fifth-floor classroom with a thud. This was bibliography class, one of the first classes in my doctoral program at Juilliard, where I learned there was a "right" way to use the library, came to know the maniacal torture device that is the Chicago Manual of Style, and discovered that I am not the kind of person who will spend their days writing scholarly texts about music.

Our bibliography teacher, Professor J, the head librarian and doctoral program head, encouraged me. She tailored resources and examples in class specifically for me as an oboist. As if to say, *Come on, you're one of seven students we accepted;*

just because you're not a pianist or a composer, it doesn't mean you can't do this. She was a genuine and passionate advocate for us. But also insisted: *Please use original source material and be fastidious and thoroughly perfect.*

I was plenty fastidious all on my own. I sacrificed myself at the altar of perfectionism back then—this full-scholarship life should have made me feel better, but instead, the work felt like one big guilt offering to a God I feared hated me. I tried to memorize when to use a comma versus parentheses in citations. I exerted all my energy to complete every assignment on time and with a smile. I learned every rule and its nine hundred exceptions. With each mistake that still slipped in, and even when I succeeded in producing a perfect citation list, I felt more and more crestfallen. I had this sense I was living across the street from my dream, watching it go by each day from where I sat up high above Broadway.

How do we end up in these shadow versions of our lives? In his book *Turning Pro*, Steven Pressfield coined the term "shadow careers" for the pursuit of the thing adjacent to the dream itself, the job that is similar to your true calling but not quite it. He posits that when we get a job as a graphic designer instead of becoming a painter—when we choose something that is just to the right of our actual dream—it might be due to our fear of failure or success.

I was hungry for some kind of confirmation that I belonged, so I worked hard to get noticed by my teachers, to astonish everyone, and to be "the best." I was ravenous but also full—of "food" I did not find satisfying in the least. And in bibliography class, no shade to Professor J, I was hopelessly, irretrievably, and comprehensively bored. Instead of taking this as a sign I might not be on the right path, I felt like a scared animal, trapped and ashamed.

Our Many Names

I grew up as "Meri" in rural South Carolina—a place that loves its nicknames—but I dreamed of living in New York and being an artist. My grandparents had introduced my sister and me to the Big Apple (or The City). The details of my exact ambition were unclear back then; I just knew how I wanted to feel.

I'd spend hours singing show tunes to the mirror with our brand-new CD player in the living room when no one was home. I'd lie on the floor of my bedroom listening to Aaron Copland's "Appalachian Spring" and attempt to inhabit the open chords and spacious harmonies. I longed to see the world, to know what made this music so beautiful. When Copland's finale came on, with its lilting folk melody, I would rise from the floor and move my body with the brass, feeling goosebumps across my arms. *This* was how I wanted to feel: free. I wanted to fill my life with this feeling, whatever it took.

And so, when I learned that I wasn't bad at playing the oboe—an instrument equal parts strange and unapologetically heartfelt, not unlike my own temperament at that age—I figured this was my ticket. I set my sights on Juilliard because it was in New York and because I had heard people say that it was "the best." When I left for boarding school at sixteen, my mother began calling me "Birdy" because I was always flying away. Each step I took toward the dream held great expectation: to feel qualified and ready to call myself a musician, an oboist, a conservatory graduate.

Imagine my confusion when, a decade or so later, near the end of the first semester of my doctoral program, I heaved myself into the by-then familiar four walls of bibliography class, venti Starbucks in hand, felt the heavy door seal behind me, and it was mostly dread I felt, not joy. We were all hoping to add "scholar" to the list of qualifiers in our bios, but each day I spent in pursuit of that title, left me feeling more and more lost.

As I sat down beneath the shadow of all those great musicians who had sat in my seat before me, I heard a question, one that up until this point in the school year I had been ignoring, ringing in my ears so loudly I could barely breathe: *What are you doing here?*

A Secret Playbook

As she did for every class, Professor J had rolled a large cart of hardback volumes, taller than she was, from her office in the library to our classroom down the hall. She held up each one and explained its purpose in our future dissertation research. Her arms quivered from the weight of a burgundy volume with gold lettering that she announced was a bibliography of bibliographies—a meta-bibliography. As we feigned interest over a book listing other books, she came to her last piece of research material to show us that day.

"These are tune indexes, annotated lists of melodies," she said. "Flip through them and find something familiar." She shared that musicologists have been naming and cataloging tunes for centuries. In hymnody—the study of hymn singing—these indexes are lists of melodies, officially named, followed by information about the song's various text settings, other titles they may have been known by, and a brief historical blurb. Other musical traditions and instrumental repertoires have indexes, too. (Let's be real: there is probably a meta-index, an index of tune indexes, but you'd have to go to the library and find that out for yourself!)

When it was my turn to open the dusty, linen-bound book, I felt goosebumps on my arm. I wasn't sure why.

As I began turning the pages, I felt like I had stumbled upon some top-secret playbook. Melodies I'd sung all my life had new strange names: Amazing Grace = New Britain, Praise God from Whom All Blessings Flow = Old Hundredth. *What were these names, and what did they mean?* This book spoke another language; it cast a hopeful light.

"St. Anne," I read, "with the most popular text, 'Our God, our help in ages past.' Named for St. Anne's Cathedral in London where the tune's composer William Croft was organist."

"Eventide," I read, "the tune for the hymn 'Abide with Me,' the name evocative of the peace of twilight." While some tunes were named after the first line of their most popular setting ("Adeste Fideles" is the tune name for "O Come All Ye Faithful," for example), most of the official names I read in the index, even of familiar songs, were new to me.

I felt Professor J's eyes on me. I was worried I may have been taking too long, that I should pass the book to my colleague on the right, and turned one last page. That's when I saw it. An entry for a tune that called to me in the shadows:

> Simple Gifts: shaker melody from 1848, used most notably in Aaron Copland's "Appalachian Spring" and innumerable iterations throughout the 20th century, including a hymn entitled "Lord of the Dance" included in many Protestant hymnals. Often sung slower and more stately, this tune was originally conceived as a dance in Shaker worship, labeled "quick dance" in early manuscripts.

Here was my beloved "Appalachian Spring," only now it was revealed to me by its true name, accompanied by all the other forms it had assumed over the years. The first arrangement I'd ever heard was Copland's—the classical, symphonic setting with noble brass and shimmering strings. I realized then I'd sung the same melody from the dark red hymnal at Main Street United Methodist Church, this time entitled, "Lord of the Dance." I remembered how, after worship, my older brother would scream-sing the tune with made-up words from the top of the stairs in his shaky pubescent voice until the whole family laughed. Now, I sat in a classroom in the middle of New York

City, and here it was again, this time by its real name, "Simple Gifts." This dance tune composed by a small religious sect in nineteenth-century rural Maine had become my own personal rhapsody, weaving a strangely synchronous tapestry, given to an oboist across time and space. A musical gift, as simple as they come, was so much more to me than a quick entry in an index could name.

As I held this book and I looked down at the different names for this melody that had spoken to me all those years ago, I sensed, again but like for the first time, a kind of belovedness, a benevolence, not just for the gift of this music and the musicologists who collected and cherished these melodies, but for my Creator, who, I realized at that moment, had named me before anyone else, was collecting me in all my iterations, and was *loving* me, too.

As I felt the pages of that seemingly ancient book against my fingers, as I sat with all my questions about my future as a musician, writer, and scholar, as I saw "Simple Gifts" listed there—a tune I'd loved in every form, no less beautiful or joyful in an orchestra hall, a sunlit church, or coming from a silly (slightly irreverent) teenager's mouth—I imagined God singing us into existence.

The Melodic Heart of God

As a child, my mother would enter my room to wake me with a melodic "rise and shine," and even just thinking of it now, singing her melody to myself, I feel her delighting in me. I don't always live like I'm worth singing over, or that my Creator not only fights my battles but also delights in me with rhapsodic joy and gives me my own life-song to sing.

The prophet Zephaniah says, "The Lord, your God, is in your midst, a warrior who gives victory; he will rejoice over you with gladness; he will renew you in his love; he will exult over you with loud singing" (Zephaniah 3:17).

Life has its way with us; we make our way in this heart-wrenching world, singing the songs of our lives as best we know how, only to wake up and realize we've lost the theme. I learned that day in bibliography class that every tune has a name, and my composer knows mine.

Your True Name

Have you looked for others in your life to name you? To give you a sense of identity and value? How's that been working out for you?

We long to see our lives as a trajectory, a linear progression like a neat, three-line entry in a hardback volume, when really what we are is a melody, written and rewritten, up-tempo and down, transposed and reharmonized through time, called many names, some that fit better than others. Maybe all your life, you've been trying to sing your life's song with an orchestra behind you when you're really an unpretentious barn dancer. Maybe you thought you could only be defined by what you do, like a tune named for the first line of its text, but in reality, you are more than your performance, more than the roles you play, your true name hiding somewhere beneath the shiny surface. Maybe you somehow ended up in a degree program for scholars when what you really wanted was to play the oboe and to write essays and poems about spirituality and art.

Merideth, Meri, Birdy, Oboist, Writer, Mama—I've gone by many names, and I'd bet you have too. We move through life's roles and seasons, stretching to fit a new container, adding brass here and developing an interesting counterpoint there, but no matter the setting, no matter the U-turns, no matter the instrumentation, we are named Beloved. Like every great melody, there will be times you'll hardly recognize yourself as you go through a particularly rough episode of development, when you're thrown from one instrument to another. It can be disorienting, bewildering, discouraging. What if, no matter the role you play or career detour you take there is something unshakably true about you, available through the simple gift of God's love, which vibrates in every interval? A song whose name only God knows? What if all the complexity and confusion of your busy life can't change the simple fact that you are worthy of love, just as you are? And what if that fact could set you free?

The lyrics are true. It is the gift to be simple; it is the gift to be free. I remember reading in my research that the lyrics are often mistakenly written with "a" instead of "the." It is not *a* gift to be simple but *the* gift. The gift is simplicity. The gift is freedom. This is what loving God means. It is not something we do; it is something we are given. Our identities—beloved and inherently worthy—are not earned but gifted to us. We can stand up and walk out of the shadow lives and step into our truest and most aligned orchestrations, trusting that no matter how many times we turn, no matter how many wrong harmonizations we may find ourselves in, there is a composer who sings over us, delights in us, and calls us by name.

The Place Just Right

Like ear training, I think I passed bibliography class with a B minus. After graduation, when I was named Associate Professor (another setting that was only right for me for a time), I spent years feeling guilty that I wasn't writing and publishing scholarly articles and contributing to that particular pool of meaning. Now I know that scholarly publication wasn't my song to sing. What a relief! I found my way out of the shadows, not by shaming myself into a place I wasn't meant to be, but by trusting *the* original source, the One with the meta-narrative, a larger, higher vision than we can see. God knows how the grand symphony of my life sounds; I do not write it as I go. I get to discover it and sing along.

What looked at first like fragmentation and cacophonous chaos, what I thought was a tragic breaking apart, was really my life's song being broken open.

I want to remind you of what I learned from bibliography class and my temporary obsession with tune indexes: that something as unique and precious as a melody, with its lilt or intensity, its symmetry or surprising elisions, hard as we might try, cannot be contained in a category or inventory. As much as we'd like to analyze and understand what makes it great, to transpose, reharmonize, and orchestrate it differently—there comes a point in all of our intellectualizing when there is only one thing left to do: sing.

Go live that life that is *yours*. And when you forget your melody, when you long to find yourself in the place just right (and fear you're not), when you're tempted to rush on ahead instead of listening and waiting for the mysterious beauty of a new verse to unfold, may you go to your Great Composer, the one who makes the morning stars sing together (Job 38:7) the one who, in his human form, sang a hymn of praise even in the face of death (Matthew 26:30). Step out of the shadow and into the light of the One who has overcome the darkness. Ask this One to help you receive the simplest gift: the freedom that comes with hearing your composer call your name, singing over you with uncontainable, exuberant delight.

ARS NOVA

Let Art Sing Your Soul's Song

1. Name some of the roles you play and list some of the different ways you use your energies and gifts. These can be both practical and more conceptual, past tense or roles you play now. (e.g., mother, the dependable one, the housekeeper, the musician, the Juilliard grad, the

middle child) Characterize yourself in this first list by considering how you relate to others and the specific parts you play or things you've done in your life.

2. Now, write about a time in the past when you felt most like yourself. How old were you? What were you doing that connected you to being who you are? What did you like most about yourself in this memory? (e.g., Singing show tunes in the mirror when no one was home. Something about music was transcendent and joyful. I liked the power and heart in my voice. I liked that I wasn't afraid. I like that I was free.)
3. Lastly, make a new list naming who you are outside of the roles you play or the things you do. Attempt to strip away your socialization, the names others have given you and look at what sociologist Martha Beck calls your "Essential Self," the person you are or would be when no one is watching, when you are not acting out of duty or toward some larger goal. (e.g., dreamer, tender-hearted, lover of laughter, performer)
4. Choose a work of art from any medium that captures a word or two from your second list. If you need ideas, try searching keywords from your list with the word "art." Listen to or view the work of art of choice every day for one week. Reflect on what God might be teaching you about your unique expression of an artist's love.

Chapter 6

Art Is a Burning Bush

Faith Ringgold, "Picasso's Studio" (1991)

Moses was keeping the flock of his father-in-law Jethro, the priest of Midian; he led his flock beyond the wilderness and came to Mount Horeb, the mountain of God. There the angel of the Lord appeared to him in a flame of fire out of a bush; he looked, and the bush was blazing, yet it was not consumed. Then Moses said, "I must turn aside and look at this great sight and see why the bush is not burned up." When the Lord saw that he had turned aside to see, God called to him out of the bush, "Moses, Moses!" And he said, "Here I am." Then he said, "Come no closer! Remove the sandals from your feet, for the place on which you are standing is holy ground." He said further, "I am the God of your father, the God of Abraham, the God of Isaac, and the God of Jacob." And Moses hid his face, for he was afraid to look at God.

Then the Lord said, "I have observed the misery of my people who are in Egypt; I have heard their cry on account of their taskmasters. Indeed, I know their sufferings, and I have come down to deliver them from the Egyptians and to bring them up out of that land to a good and spacious land, to a land flowing with milk and honey, to the country of the Canaanites, the Hittites, the Amorites, the Perizzites, the Hivites, and the Jebusites. The cry of the Israelites has now come to me; I have also seen how the Egyptians oppress them. Now go, I am sending you to Pharaoh to bring my people, the Israelites, out of Egypt." But Moses said to God, "Who am I that I should go to Pharaoh and bring the Israelites out

> of Egypt?" He said, "I will be with you, and this shall be the sign for you that it is I who sent you: when you have brought the people out of Egypt, you shall serve God on this mountain."
>
> But Moses said to God, "If I come to the Israelites and say to them, 'The God of your ancestors has sent me to you,' and they ask me, 'What is his name?' what shall I say to them?" God said to Moses, "I am who I am." He said further, "Thus you shall say to the Israelites, 'I am has sent me to you.'"
>
> —Exodus 3:1–14

> You asked me once why I wanted to become an artist and I said I didn't know. Well I know now. It is because it's the only way I know of feeling free.
>
> —Faith Ringgold

It was fall when I first rode with Nan. As we turned off the interstate and into the neighborhood, I gasped. "Whoa. What *is* that?"

"That's *Euonymus alatus*," she said, "a.k.a. Burning Bush."

The shrubs that Nan nodded toward shone a brilliant orange at the top of an abandoned street like a welcome—or a warning. As we crossed into the derelict, desolate neighborhood just off Seven Mile, October's palette was a cruel irony. The vibrant crimson reds of sugar oaks and maples, the orange and yellows of other trees I couldn't name, were reflected in the broken windows of hollowed-out homes as if they were shattered mirrors, the weary shoulders of their porches sagging like they'd given up. The natural beauty of fall was draped across the loss and decay of a neighborhood abandoned. As we pulled into this seemingly forsaken place, I wondered if I was about to have my own burning bush moment, if I was about to meet God here, of all places.

Nan was my chauffeur for this mission into a crumbled community in North Detroit with a known human trafficking problem. A former law enforcement officer turned inner-city missionary, Nan was a fierce woman, small and strong, with short, spiky, silver hair. She donned long earrings made of feathers and rocked a lipstick that was a shade or two more purple than I'd ever been brave enough to wear. I'd met her a week or so earlier at a church event where she'd spoken about her work. She'd explained that many squat in these homes all year with no heat and broken windows, without power and/or running water. Traffickers pursue the most vulnerable—women *and* men, teens, even children—through online channels and in person at hotels or motels and lure them to neighborhoods like these. They charm them into drug addiction and use them for sex trafficking, treating humans like they are disposable commodities to be consumed.

I had heard of all this before, but when I heard Nan speak, my heart was shattered anew. When she said off-hand at the end of her talk that she was looking for two more adults to ride along to deliver supplies and food to victims of human trafficking as soon as next Friday, I found myself, almost involuntarily, raising my hand.

Give Me Your Worst

Riding into the worst neighborhoods of my new city only months after moving there seemed like a reasonable idea, kind of like when you tell someone on a first date everything you've ever done to see how they react. *OK, Detroit, give me your worst. I'd like to know what I'm getting into.* As much as I did want to serve alongside Nan, I was also using this outing as a means to avoid my life. We'd moved when I was eight months pregnant, and now that we were settling in and the baby was starting to crawl, it was finally time to get back to work creating. Every time

I sat down to write, I had nothing to say. Each time I grabbed my instrument for practice, it felt like holding a foreign object. The days felt long and the nights were a monotonous, parallel universe of breastfeeding and watching Eli sleep. I still woke up disoriented, unsure of where I was. The echo chamber of postpartum anxiety left me feeling simultaneously touched-out and incredibly lonely, consumed by fears that I'd never feel like myself again, that I'd never get my skill or energy back, that this new place would never feel like home. Once, while driving downriver, I passed the "Bridge to Canada" sign and said out loud to an empty car, "What am I doing here?" This is my favorite question to ask myself in listless, unsettling times.

In an attempt to answer that question, I'd called a babysitter, thawed some milk from my freezer stash, and gone to meet Nan.

In her van, I adjusted my seatbelt, pulling it away from my neck. As we hit another pothole, I realized just how unsettled my soul felt.

It all made sense to me now, why Moses would run away into the desert.

Waiting for TJ

Nan's driving was calm, yet expeditious. Turning on a local radio station that played an old Motown song I didn't know, she seemed to belong here in a way I didn't. As a former cop, she knew a lot about the city. She had been at raids where they arrested adults and freed minors who were being exploited. When she'd become a mother, she decided to leave the raids to the police, and instead, start a non-profit that worked to be in fellowship with those in the cycle of addiction and abuse—to develop relationships, especially with the women, to invite them to trust someone on the outside so they might one day walk away into freedom.

"Why don't they just jump in the van and come to the shelter with you?" The woman in the front seat asked, speaking loudly over the music.

Nan answered, "You can't make someone want to leave. But at some point, it will become scarier to stay than it is to walk away. That's the moment I'm waiting for."

Before that day, I figured that most of the people in human trafficking rings were actively being held against their will. Many are, and this is where local law enforcement and even the FBI come in, freeing victims and arresting the ring leaders of these horrendous operations. Nan explained that many victims ensnared in such evil cycles, especially women, when given a chance to escape, feel they cannot walk away. I learned that many have opportunities to voluntarily escape, and yet even when their captors are lax about security and the literal chains are loosened, they choose to stay.

Nan had told us about some of the people we would meet. One woman was the daughter of a University of Michigan professor, who'd fallen into drugs, and no matter what they tried, her family couldn't get her out and sober. They'd finally given up looking for her, assuming she was dead. Another had been an orphaned teen who'd run away from an abusive foster parent and been picked up by a drug dealer who gave her her first hit of heroin. I caught Nan's eyes in the van's large rearview mirror. "She believed this man was the first and only person to ever love her, and so why would she leave him?"

This is an insidious aspect of human trafficking: treating people as disposable commodities for long enough eventually makes them believe they are disposable commodities. Nan knew that to free people from the evils of human trafficking, they needed more than raids, more than opportunity; they needed love. We had to invite them into another life, help them believe they belonged, convince them they are worthy to live it.

I swallowed the lump forming in my throat. As we pulled up to a home that looked more like a demolition site, Nan put the van in park, and I tried hard not to look away.

It was a brick house with boards for windows, a hole for a chimney. The matted grass had folded over onto itself and died. Because they knew Nan and expected her every Tuesday and Friday, two women with sunken eyes soon emerged from the dwelling. From the back of Nan's van, we passed out pre-made bags of hygiene care, fresh leggings and socks, and sandwiches made by church members, while Nan greeted them with a genuine smile. Eventually, two men appeared. They barely spoke or met our gaze. We handed the male version of the hygiene kit through the window, and they almost immediately sulked back into the house silently. I tried to smile as my heart pounded. The van felt stuffy. I noticed Nan frequently looking in the rearview mirror.

At our second or third house, Nan lingered longer than she had at the others. "I'm waitin' for TJ." We were all silent, too afraid to ask or learn the newest heartbreaking details.

"Most of the time," Nan explained, "we pass out supplies, we chat with the women, and then we leave. But occasionally, someone will need a doctor—they'll ask for a ride to the hospital. They'll beg me not to call an ambulance, call attention to the house." She paused. We all kept watching the door. "And sometimes . . . very rarely . . ." her voice lowering almost to a whisper, "they decide they're ready to *leave*. They want to get clean and move to one of the shelters or transitional housing. And when they're ready, we'll take 'em."

After what felt like an hour of my eyes darting from the door of TJ's house to each of the rearview mirrors and back, after I had lost and caught my breath with each car with tinted windows that had passed us by, a young woman no older than twenty emerged from the dark hole of a house.

"Here she comes," Nan scream-whispered, "Open the door." My eyes widened for a second; I wasn't sure I heard her correctly. For everyone else, we'd just passed the supplies through the window, but as I saw Nan's expectant face shining from up front, I reached across the aisle, pulled the handle, and slid the heavy black door open for TJ.

She walked slowly toward us, determined yet cautious. TJ—short for Tori Jean, I later learned—looked weary and worn, but there was a light in her eyes, however dim. Her face was puffy and ashen, her skin almost translucent, covering her narrow frame like a veil. Her protruding ribs, which I could count through her skin-tight tank top, rose and fell like the wings of an elegant bird. Her teeth were brown and broken, but she smiled like you do at your favorite teacher. She wore a necklace with a braided cord and a small black cross, which rested deep into her pushed-up cleavage. I wondered if this cross was a gift from Nan. There was small talk; Nan introduced us. I took off my sunglasses so I could look her right in the eyes. I tried to really see her.

There was discussion of a woman in TJ's house who'd been missing; she still hadn't resurfaced. In the silence, I heard their fear that she was dead. TJ took her bag of food and hygiene kit, and she pulled out a granola bar, eating it right there at the van's open door.

"Ya know," she said between bites, "one of these days, Ms. Nan," pausing, chewing, "I'm goin' come with ya."

Nan was calm and didn't break eye contact. "Oh yeah? Why don't you get in the van right now?"

I watched TJ breathe; she swallowed and wiped her mouth with her forearm. Cleared her throat. She closed her eyes for a moment, looked to her right, and then down.

I frantically put my sunglasses back on as tears fell and soaked my skin. *What are we doing here?*

At the top of the block, the bushes burned unseen.

Meeting God at Moma

I once saw a terrifying painting at the Museum of Modern Art in New York City by Pablo Picasso, titled *Les*

Demoiselles d'Avignon, which means *The Young Women of Avignon Street.* Many say this was the first cubist painting, and in fun-house-mirror style, Picasso depicts five nude women from a brothel he frequented, posing around a bowl of fruit with faces of African masks and Iberian sculptures, disfigured bodies, eerie blank stares. The placard said this work of art had "profoundly influenced the development of modern art." When I stood in the museum before this work, I felt deeply uncomfortable and sad. It seemed to say something extreme about the male gaze, cultural appropriation, and human consumption. Something dark and hopeless.

In what felt like the next room of the museum, I found that same image of Picasso's embedded into a story quilt by Faith Ringgold, now ablaze with a divine message. In Ringgold's version, like each quilt in her *French Collection*, the artist depicts fictional Willia Marie, a young African-American girl from Atlanta, who travels to 1920s Paris to interact with great artists and writes home about her experiences. "Picasso's Studio" shows Willia herself modeling for Picasso in *Les Demoiselles d'Avignon*, and by putting herself into the picture, she rewrites history.

In the handwritten letter to her aunt that flanks the quilt's edges, Willia says, "I really think modeling is boring. Standing, sitting or laying down. You may know what to do with your hands, your feet, the look on your face. But what do you do with your mind, with your misplaced or mistaken identité? What do you do with time? Et l'artiste [and the artist], what do you feel about him?. . . First they take the body, then the soul. Or maybe it is the soul and then the body. The sequence doesn't matter, when one goes the other usually follows close behind."

Painting herself among the African masks of her ancestors that Picasso and other fine artists at the time had culturally appropriated, Ringgold seems to be saying: *Picasso, do you see me? Do you see the living likeness of these stolen faces, standing here in your studio?*

Ringgold writes this imaginary conversation to take issue with Picasso's depiction and appropriation of her culture. They called (and some still do today) the allocation of these elements in art "primitivism" and "savagery," deeming them lesser, subhuman and therefore, fit for consumption. What a metaphor, that the first cubist painting—the style that feels like a fractured and distorted version of reality—depicts women who were only as valuable as their bodies were for consuming.

Yet Picasso doesn't get to have the last word. Through Willia, Faith Ringgold picks up the conversation and demands that Picasso see her. Whereas Picasso's painting kidnaps his subjects and their culture, using them for his own advancement, Ringgold's quilt takes back their agency and, therefore, their dignity. Along the top border of the quilt, Willia writes, "You asked me once why I wanted to become an artist and I said I didn't know. Well I know now. It is because it's the only way I know of feeling free."

Her quilt was an answer to her own questions, a call to action for the Picassos of the world, and for me. That day at MoMa, Ringgold's quilt was a burning bush, singing of freedom.

Standing before it, I felt tempted to take off my shoes, for I was on holy ground. It wasn't until years later, in the van with Nan, that I realized what this theophany—this visit from the divine—meant.

Get into the Van

In the encounter with the burning bush, Moses found himself face to face with God's invitation to get into the van, to walk out of brokenness and into the creative task of leadership. His mission was simple: Return to Egypt and tell Pharaoh to let the Hebrew people go. It took a miracle to get his attention. Still, Moses doubts his calling, doubts that he has what it takes to get the people to trust him. God replies, "Tell them I AM sent you."

The miracle in this story is not that the bush is on fire (this was a known occurrence for some shrubs in the desert), but that it was not consumed in that fire. Through it, the force behind being itself, shows us that this fire is not one that consumes, but one that sets us free.

God still speaks through burning bushes, through creations ablaze with God's glory. We stand at the open doors of life, but we hesitate, believing ourselves unworthy. We think it's too late. We see all that has been stolen from us, all that we still shoulder, and we wonder: What is the point of going on, anyway?

We are all TJ. Sometimes we are even Picasso, contributing to and perpetuating harmful practices and oppressive ideals. We are trapped in the lies we believe about ourselves and the brokenness around us. We believe we can only be one thing, mother or artist, oboist or writer, sinner or saint, all the while missing the open van doors calling us to freedom, to true fulfillment in our own belovedness.

But we are all Willia, too. We are part of this conversation that is art, that is creation. In the last section of the letter that surrounds the quilt, Willia's aunt answers her many questions about the power of art and her mission: "Willia Marie, modeling ain't so-o boring . . . you have to talk to masks and paintings. The only thing you have to do is create art of importance to YOU. Show us a new way to look at life."

Quilts weave together the scraps of cloth, the discards that seem to serve no purpose, and in Ringgold's case, this is a powerful metaphor for the new stories we get to tell through the power of creation. Freedom, then, looks like reclaiming our space. It looks like rewriting the story one quilt block at a time. It looks like getting in when the van pulls up, making people see you for more than your body's value, believing you are beloved, a creation that is of great importance to God. For me, it meant asking for help, getting started again as a musician and writer; it meant building a life in Detroit, a place I now love. Even though it was scary, it meant trusting that God would take me home.

I imagine TJ believed the people in that house were her only hope, her family. It was dark and painful and scary inside, but to her, I imagine it was scary inside a van of middle-aged Christian ladies, too. In these moments, vacillating between clarity and confusion, we catch our reflection in the car window, and we consider: Would it hurt more to stay or to go?

It's not too late to get into the van. To face the fallout that will come, to change your mind, to tell the truth. It's not too late to apologize or to speak up, to make them hear you, to let God's grace chase you down into whatever derelict neighborhood or harmful patterns of self-hatred and anxiety you find yourself living in. It's not too late to escape the self-sabotaging tendencies you have to burn down your life, and instead, pick up the brush. Let God's creative love sew together the disparate scraps of this life into a beautiful, complex quilt of stories that our Creator is still weaving.

The spiritual song of created things cries of freedom. It is a fire—a grace—that does not consume but leads us beyond our small plans and tidy suburbs, beyond the limited and twisted ways we see each other as objects to consume, and sets us free. Creating anything is scary, but creating a life out of the brokenness of your current one—picking up the brush and taking your place in the painting, rewriting a narrative, getting into the van—this can be the scariest of all.

Here I Am

TJ did not get in the van that day. A couple of weeks later, there was some violence in the neighborhood that made it too dangerous for Nan to ride, and I lost touch with her and all the women I met that day.

We go to the margins to serve others, and some of us believe (arrogantly) that we can change the world by our own strength. From the few times I rode along, I believe Nan's ministry had a lasting impact on the women of North Detroit. It feels important to acknowledge that there are so-called ministries that distort and consume those they started off trying to help, that there are examples of toxic charity that perpetuate oppression and harm. All I can say is that day, I came to the margins to possibly change a neighborhood, but it was I who was forever changed.

When I close my eyes to pray, I see the vehicle open, myself on the street, busy with my own excuses, holding on to little (and big) lies that make a lot of sense to me, in my heart, a fear that I am too broken, too unworthy of love, too late. God stands patiently at the van door, smiling gently, the flame of grace, calling me into freedom.

No matter what holds you captive, the message of the burning bush is the promise that God steps into the deserts of this world so we will not be consumed. God hears the cries of the oppressed. In the great quilt of creation, God answers Ringgold's question, "Does he see me standing in his studio?" with a resounding "Yes!" God has never and will never stop seeing you.

If, like me, you find yourself asking, *What am I doing here?*, know first that you are asking the right question. Then, look up. Look for the bits of creation God has set ablaze for you, to call you into greater purpose.

When I looked into TJ's eyes, I realized that if God can use Moses, a fearful murderer, then God can certainly use me. That means God can use you, too. You have a brush—or a pen or a flute or a wheel—that will tell the stories we haven't heard yet, that will show us a new way to look at life. And what a miracle to be an artist, to be used as one of the flawed human voices of God's creation, to walk others toward freedom.

May we follow Faith Ringgold's lead, take up our brush, and make ourselves seen. May we say, "Here I am," when we hear the call of the oppressed.

May our art be a burning bush, lighting the way to the One who sets us free.

ARS NOVA

Let Art Burn Bright

Find a work of art that helps you hear the cry of the oppressed. Below are a few examples from the civil rights movement in the United States that I have found especially powerful.

- *The French Collection*, story quilts of Faith Ringgold
- *The Migration Series*, a group of paintings by Jacob Lawrence
- *Uncle Tom's Cabin*, a novel by Harriet Beecher Stowe
- *The Fire Next Time*, essays by James Baldwin
- "Two Black Churches," music for baritone and orchestra by Shawn E. Okpebholo
- "To a Brown Girl Dead," song by Margaret Bonds, poem by Countee Cullen

Reflect on the power of art as a burning bush.

1. How does art especially help us to understand others' experiences?
2. After viewing, reading, or hearing one or more of these works of art, what feels important now?
3. How can you be part of setting yourself and others free?

Interlude

Artifacts

> A father to the fatherless, a defender of widows, is God in his holy dwelling.
>
> —Psalm 68:5 NIV

Of course, it is from a dwelling place that God defends widows, because—in my experience—that's where you find them, standing alone in theirs, with all the *stuff.*

"He would love for you to have it."

She hung the leather jacket of her late husband over my husband's shoulders like a christening.

As the wife of a pastor, the shadow of death brushes by us more than most. After homemade soup, in the silent house, save the grandfather clock, she'd disappeared to their bedroom and reemerged with the jacket.

These rooms had become, like every room after a death, an archeology. She stood back and checked the fit with a sorrowful strength.

"Are you sure?" My husband said, looking in the hallway mirror. It was big, but perfect.

How do worn-down armchairs and illegible grocery lists and smudged reading glasses become art?

Artifacts, from the Latin *arte factum*, means "something made with skill."

What we make—with gardening gloves still black with earth, with scarves and leather jackets and work suits and socks—is a life.

How does the side of a bed become a sacred relic?

It's Love that does it: The sacred song of created things vibrates with the tenderness of a Maker who has the skill to make even dust beloved.

If these artifacts are proof of life, each wrinkle a fossil—if, when loved, a chipped mug becomes a holy vessel—if ordinary things are given meaning because of who they belong to, then how much more are we treasured, made precious, by the Love that made us?

> You have collected all my tears in a bottle. (Psalm 56:8 NLT)

Now, I'm starting to understand that standing amid God's artifacts, being one myself, in these temporary dwellings, collecting tears, taking the jacket—is holy work.

Chapter 7

Clay Sculptor
Ruth Duckworth, The Creation (1983)

> I think of life as a unity. This includes mountains, mice, rocks, trees, women, and men. It's all one big lump of clay.
>
> —Ruth Duckworth

As we pulled into Dachau, I felt all the different iterations of myself rattling around in my heart, like one of those ceramic nesting dolls.

The sun shone with an almost cruel clarity, highlighting the stark reality of the camp against the backdrop of new life. Fleeting bursts of light broke through the blooming birch trees, attempting to brighten a place forever shadowed.

Our tour guide announced that the eighty-year anniversary of the liberation of the camp was just two days prior. Here we were, at the very first concentration camp of the Nazis, used as a model for all the others, while from the ground stained by immense evil and suffering came abundant, green shoots of grass, hopeful like some long-silenced chorus.

This particular trip to Germany, part of my husband's work as pastor and spiritual pilgrimage leader, focused on the Protestant Reformation, music, and World War II history. As soon as we landed and my German language skills came pouring back, I realized that returning to this place came with an amorphous, emotional ball of memories from my year as a Fulbright Scholar at a small music conservatory in the Black Forest—much too heavy for my carry-on.

I'd arrived on this country's doorstep all those years ago—called last minute off the wait list for the Fulbright U.S. Student program—searching for something, some version of myself, that I never found. The person I was when I'd lived in Germany was a knotted-up, self-involved, self-doubting girl, looking for some purpose, some big break that she feared would never come. The ghost of Merideths past wandered the streets of the picturesque and storied German towns; these were parts of me I hadn't thought about in decades.

During my Fulbright year, I'd once sat on a train station platform for hours, waiting for someone who never came. There'd been a beauty in the solitude, but a searing pain, too. Back then, I remember longing for some confirmation that I was good enough, that I would "make it" as an oboist, that I would know that I was OK. I performed my degree recitals, and even though I passed and was granted the Artist Diploma, I rushed into the one-room apartment where I lived alone and wept. I had this stinging feeling that somehow, I had failed. I left with new musical facility and knowledge, and even deeper insecurity and the same profound sadness that felt like a crack through a perfectly nice vase.

The girl I was back then would never have thought to visit a concentration camp. Nor would she have set foot within the cathedrals or other places of spiritual or historical significance unless it was a Fulbright-sponsored trip or requirement. She was not unfeeling, just a bit disinterested in others' suffering, self-centered, but from a place of deep insecurity, trepidatiously exploring her newfound freedom of being away from everything familiar. Some part of her also knew she didn't have the faith to face real tragedy or encounter the big questions. God was a box best left closed. She kept her head down and worked hard to win worthiness by being perfect.

That girl had meandered through her small village, to and from the practice rooms, amid the beautiful forest foliage, pausing at the edge of the woods to ask existential questions of a God she wasn't sure existed.

What is the meaning of this life?
Am I working so hard just to be given the chance to work even harder in the future?
Is this striving all there is?
Where are you, God?

The weight of these and other questions had loomed like dark clouds in the landscape of early adulthood. Each facet of the music career that she dreamed of and each relationship she pursued felt empty, a path leading to a cavernous, hollow echo.

She left Germany without the confirmation she'd longed for; her questions of suffering met with silence.

Being Clay

The prophet Isaiah, in chapter 64, offers a prayer of lament and confession to the people of Judah, newly returned to Jerusalem after the Babylonian exile, in approximately the eighth century BCE. Amid the pleas for God to intervene and show power to the nations, amid feelings of unworthiness and mourning, he says, "Yet, O Lord, you are our Father; we are the clay, and you are our potter; we are all the work of your hand" (Isaiah 64:8).

A century or so later, the prophet Jeremiah receives a similar message, on his own pilgrimage: "This is the word that came to Jeremiah from the Lord: 'Go down to the potter's house, and there I will give you my message.' So I went down to the potter's house, and I saw him working at the wheel. But the pot he was shaping from the clay was marred in his hands; so the potter formed it into another pot, shaping it as seemed best to him. Then the word of the Lord came to me. He said, 'Can I not do with you, Israel, as this potter does?' declares the Lord. 'Like clay in the hand of the potter, so are you in my hand, Israel'" (Jeremiah 18, 1–6 NIV). This image of being clay in the hands of God for ancient Jewish listeners would have connected immediately to Genesis 1 where, in creation, God fashioned man "from the dust of the ground." God called him Adam, a name derived from the Hebrew word *adamah*, which means "ground," "soil," or "dirt."

These Scriptures show God as an artist again, hunched over the potter's wheel, hands dirty. These prophecies show God's creative power and sovereignty over us, our Creator's willingness to see the potential of formless clay, to design and shape us with delicate patience. The word for "work" in the Isaiah passage is connected to the Greek word *poemia*, from Ephesians 2. We are the work of God's hands, the craftsmanship, masterwork, creation, the work of a Master Artist. (This will be our topic in chapter 11.)

In Jeremiah's vision, the focus is on the malleability of the clay, that we have not been hardened or left yet for the fiery kiln, but that God is still active in creating us, forming us, this is the power of God at the potter's wheel. God's hands are centering the clay on the wheel with focus. Our Maker feels the life, the potential, in each damp mound. With patience and a strong hand, our shape and purpose are formed by One who loves us. In Genesis, God made beautiful things out of dirt, and that process has never stopped. We are still being formed and transformed.

But what do these Scriptures mean at the gates of Dachau?

Our travel companions on this particular tour were committed congregants of my husband's church, plus individuals from other congregations who loved the fellowship of pilgrimage. Edwin and I were the age of most of the pilgrims' children. Some were old enough to have parents who had fought in WWII; all of them vividly remembered when the Berlin Wall came down, the topic of our tour the week prior. One pilgrim had brought pictures and letters from her father, who had liberated another concentration camp in 1945.

I realized suddenly that I wasn't the only one carrying different versions of herself, the stories of her own life and the lives of others, within her. As I caught my reflection in the window of the bus, I imagined it: my different selves fitting snugly into one another, my soul growing slowly in size with the addition of each new doll, my Potter reforming me. I knew the shape of my life was an entirely different-sized vessel now. Now my heart felt as wide as a bowl. As much as I'd tried to prepare myself for this experience, I felt my selves expanding again. I knew I was leaving an old version of me behind.

At the gates of Dachau, I was grateful for this sense of expansion, yet the questions I had for God last time I was in Germany began to bubble up again, my faith felt childlike and impossibly fragile.

The Book of Death

The plates and cups at Dachau were made of metal. No ceramics for prisoners. They were too easily broken, too simple to make into weapons.

One exhibition featured a photograph of a metal bowl with a Star of David carved into its underside. I read stories of poets and musicians and visual artists who created big and small works of art in the camps, in some cases, risking their lives to share their words, capture their despair, and hope beyond hope that God would hear their cries and rescue them.

My husband Edwin and I had decided to take our own paths through the camp, so I walked around the grounds alone. I put my headphones in and followed the dotted line on my flimsy paper map. The iron sign on the front gate of the prisoners' camp said, "Arbeit Macht Frei," which translates to "Work makes you free." The gravel crunched against my feet as I walked through it. When I entered the roll call area, a sprawling courtyard of emptiness, I looked up at the towers on all sides. I felt watched as I squinted my eyes in the brilliant sunshine of the jarringly gorgeous day.

There are many harrowing stories I will carry with me from that place. My heart broke open when I looked up at a crude-looking cement ceiling, dried concrete pouring out from the side of each brick as it pressed against the next. I could sense the pressure between each cinderblock. I realized then that the structure I was standing in was built by prisoners. As I made my way through the eerie hallways of the gas chambers and past the first crematorium and then the second larger one built just before the war ended, I found myself in the memorial room, surrounded by pictures and plaques given by the families of those lost, for Italian and French prisoners, the Roma or Sinti people, for "homosexuals" and "political dissenters," Seventh Day Adventists, who refused to the join the military, and for Jews. On the right side of the small chamber was a book. A list of over 33,500 people murdered at Dachau (those they could name, anyway). I waited for the young woman before me to finish; I leaned against the wall. My stomach was hollow; my throat burned with all the unspoken words.

When it was my turn to flip through the book, I realized I didn't know exactly what I was looking for. I didn't know the name of any particular person or relative who'd been there. But I decided to look up my maiden name, Hite, in its original German spelling, and sure enough, there it was: "Josef

Heidt, captured in Bruchsal, occupation: worker, date of death: December 21, 1944." I didn't know this man, I wasn't sure we were even related, but as I held the book in my hands, I felt the remaining shards of my heart splinter.

Of the metaphors God could use to describe the connection between artist and art, maker and creation, potter and clay suddenly seemed ancient, poignant, and painful. God painting the sky or singing a song of joy over us—these images kept God remote or slightly withdrawn. But as I stood in Dachau and thought of the Jews who tried to worship in the camps—hushed, secret Shabbat services in the bunkers—I remembered the Star of David carved into the metal bowl as a prayer, a protest. I wondered if they thought of Jeremiah's vision, Isaiah's words, promising that God loved them, that they were the work of God's hands. Held against my own, the book felt impossibly thick, its pages almost translucent. Just like that, the brittle beauty of human life was porcelain fracturing against the cold concrete floor. In the photographs of men in bunkers and prisoners at roll call, their strength was obvious, but right behind their pained eyes was the tenderness of a child.

As I exited the memorial room and made my way outside, I felt weak and angry. My eyes stung. The complexity swirled in me like a cyclone. If God is the potter, did God also fashion the instruments of such immense cruelty? Did God allow the clay to be so brutally broken and consumed in this kiln of hatred? How could a loving God allow such horrific destruction of creation? The metaphor suddenly felt inadequate in the face of such human depravity, the seemingly obvious absence of the Potter's divine intervention.

Josef Heidt died on December 21, 1944, fewer than six months before liberation.

I felt the wind against my face again as it rushed through the trees, watch towers in full bloom.

On the Seventh Day

German artist, Ruth Duckworth, was born to a Jewish mother and a Lutheran father. Her family fled to England in 1936. A well-established family in Germany, the Duckworths had next to nothing in England. Ruth got a job working as a tombstone carver in Liverpool to help the family with money. She eventually was able to study fine art and began right away to focus on sculpture. She astonished everyone as she kept wanting to work, not in bronze or marble, but in clay.

For millennia, working in clay had been thought of as a utilitarian craft, making bowls and cups, for example, designed for everyday use. Artisans of some cultures would make pottery to be used for religious rituals, but items made of clay were defined first and foremost by their purpose. Early ceramic traditions, even though they showed great skill and artistry, were considered more "craft" than "art."

Ruth Duckworth changed that. She loved composing large-scale sculptures out of clay. And she quickly realized that in order for her art to be accepted and her potential fully realized, she'd need to move to the United States, where there was exciting exploration happening in the art world in the 1950s and '60s.

My favorite work of Duckworth's is a large-scale mural entitled *The Creation*, commissioned by the Congregation Beth Israel in Hammond, Indiana. This sixteen-by-sixteen-foot stoneware mural tells the story of Genesis 1. It is a large spiral, and at the center is a dark hollow circular tile representing the "undifferentiated primordial universe," where Duckworth apparently said, "God is thinking." The spirals fan outward, and you see the sun, moon, and stars take form against wave and rock, and finally, animals, plants, and humans.

What is interesting to me about this mural is not only that it is made of clay, unlike any I'd ever seen, but also what Duckworth does with the seventh day. One of the main murals that she used as her inspiration was the cupola of Creation at St. Mark's Basilica in Venice, Italy. On the seventh day in this Byzantine-influenced medieval mosaic, God is seated on a throne, surrounded by angels. In Duckworth's seventh day, however, the form turns dark again, reminiscent of the day-one chaos, the primordial universe, the moment where God is "thinking."

Duckworth worried greatly about the climate crisis and especially about the future of animals, but as I remembered this sculpture on my day in Dachau, it felt for me like an attempt at an answer to the questions I asked in Germany, during my Fulbright year and now: If God is our potter, if God loves creation, then where is God in times of destruction, in days of brokenness and suffering?

I like Duckworth's mural because it allows the question of "Where are you, God?" to hang in the air. And yet, the very nature of the spiral is that it continues outward; like Jeremiah, Duckworth believes that creation is an ongoing process. Her version of Day Seven shows darkness like a consolation, a reminder that God weeps with us. I want to believe, to hope, that God is thinking still, that God's interactions with this brittle, broken world are not over. The art makes me wonder if this perceived primordial silence *is* an answer—an answer we must live into, as creation spins on.

In his famous letter to God "Prayer for the Days of Awe," published in *The New York Times*, Romanian Jew, prisoner at Auschwitz Concentration Camp, and Professor of Humanities Elie Wiesel writes about how he rejects the numerous arguments that others have given him explaining the Holocaust. He says, "Auschwitz must and will forever remain a question mark only: It can be conceived neither with God nor without God."

What, besides art, could give us space to live in the question marks of life, to wait in the deafening silence for an answer that may never come?

What Makes You Free

As we loaded the bus again, I kept my headphones in and played the saddest music I knew: Samuel Barber's *Adagio for Strings*, Op. 11. It felt cathartic to sit in the sorrow a little longer, to allow art to help me hold the "with" and "without-ness" of Dachau, to not look away.

I thought again of that sad girl I was in Germany, nearly twenty years earlier, who "suffered." It felt wrong to even use that word after what I'd seen at Dachau. Still, something about remembering my own pain helped me feel connected to the deeper brokenness of life in the camps; running my fingers along my own aching cracks somehow allowed me to enter into others' pain. Maybe this is what it is to be human, to be clay: When we stop crying out to God in suffering or when we discount our own experiences by comparing them to others, we miss out on the very fact of our shared splinters, our mutual vulnerability. This fragility speaks to our need for God, but also our connection with and need for one another.

I am still not clear on the answers to some of the questions I asked, then and now, about suffering, but the experience made me newly aware of my own tenderness; and that is, in and of itself, a kind of answer.

At the end of Wiesel's prayer, he says, "Let us make up, Master of the Universe. In spite of everything that happened? Yes, in spite. Let us make up: for the child in me, it is unbearable to be divorced from you so long." I knew what it was to be divorced from God. I had run from God in my own suffering, too. Yet, if Elie Wiesel, someone who'd lost so much, could decide to fight for his faith, in the midst of what he experienced, couldn't I? Maybe faith isn't a place where we come to get our questions answered, but a relationship in which we choose to stay or not.

I want to believe that God is a potter, not only crafting us into useful pots with purpose, but calling us beyond craft and into art. For me, God as potter does not mean that we, as pots, sit in the hands of a sovereign and untouchable artist, at the mercy of a powerful wheel that never stops. With this God, we would be tempted to believe what the gate said: "Work makes you free." Tempted to think we must work our way to worthiness. Instead, I like to think of God like Ruth Duckworth, taking pottery beyond our small human expectations, believing that each human life is more than a number, more than our usefulness, unique and resilient proof of God's faithfulness, even in the darkest days of history. It is less like a cup or bowl and more like a mural that pulls all the different versions of our selves together and allows the most significant questions of suffering and human failure to wait in the air to be answered.

What if all along we have been making God as potter into a tidy metaphor, finding it sufficient to imagine ourselves as a product God reshapes to eliminate flaws, when actually what we are is art? Art's goal is not to answer questions exactly, but to ask different, deeper ones.

These questions we are asking about God's perceived absence are not sinful or wrong, but a sign of a relationship; they are us choosing to see our lives with or without God, they are us at the wheel with the Master of the Universe, choosing to keep spinning, trusting, yes, in spite of everything.

Through the lens of Ruth Duckworth's work, this central metaphor of God as potter has broken me open again. As I wandered around those German villages in my twenties, as I let my heart break anew at Dachau, I was being reshaped again by my potter. And even today, with each new nesting doll, with each trial, big and small, the questions of suffering appear again. I must choose, like Wiesel, to keep writing letters to God, to stay in relationship, or not. Through it all, I expand. That process is not only a metaphor for our being made new in repentance, but a testament to God's companionship with us in lament, in the question marks of life.

The world breaks us; we are not bronze or marble after all, but clay, malleable and tender. Inside each of us is the heart of a child. We wait on the train platforms and at the memorials, and we cry out. If Ruth Duckworth's words are true, that all life is a unity, is one lump of clay, then we are related to everyone in that book of death at Dachau and even to those who committed atrocities too violent to name. We have within us, each of us, some of that same strength and some of that same capacity for evil, the ability to hope in the most hopeless of circumstances, but also to destroy. After the seventh day of creation, we want our questions to be answered and everything to be clear, but Ruth Duckworth's mural reminds us that the chaos still churns.

We are shattered and imperfect, and yet God, at the spiral wheel, creates a mural of creation that holds pain and joy together, that works even our greatest places of woundedness into art, into us. God rested on the seventh day, not out of disinterest or neglect, but to remind us that it is not work that makes us free, but God's Spirit—that we are more than a craft; that God can accomplish more in rest than we could ever do in our doing.

The spiral vision of God's world—this wheel—spins on. Even in our questions, especially in our questions, God is with us, our Maker does not look away.

God loving us as a potter loves clay means that our sorrow is holy. Isaiah's message was a prayer of lament, after all; roughly 40 percent of the psalms in the Bible are those of lamentation. We can stop treating ceramics like they aren't art; we can stop seeing our fragile and flawed nature as a deficit and trust the one who sits at the spiral. Perhaps our potter "shaping the marred pot as seemed best to him" is God breaking our hearts for what breaks the heart of God, breaking us open to hold more, to sense God's "with-ness," even when we do not hear God's voice—making us more in the image of the Maker, the image of Christ himself, whose body was broken for us.

As I turned once more to Dachau fading in the distance, I knew God was there, and here, in questions with me, and with them. I took off my sunglasses and let the spring sun shine on my puffy eyes, like wet clay submitting to be shaped again.

I don't pretend to understand God's ways, but today, I choose not to be divorced from God.

There are no neat and tidy answers—pottery is messy, after all—but there is a profound comfort in knowing we are held, even in our deepest lament, by an artist who is willing to return again and again to the wheel, hands persistent, dirty. Being the work of God's hands means taking part in the hope that can be found, rebuilt, reshaped, from the fragments of this shattered world.

ARS NOVA

Let Art Break Your Heart

Find a work of art created during or about the Holocaust. Here is a very short list of ideas to get you started.

Visual Art:

- Drawings, paintings, and sketches by prisoners: Karel Fleischmann, Peter Kien, Yehuda Bacon, Felix Nussbaum
- Art by Samuel Bak, Zoran Mušič
- Memorial to the Murdered Jews of Europe (Peter Eisenman)
- Yad Vashem—The World Holocaust Remembrance Center: Various Artists and Architects

Literature:

- *The Diary of a Young Girl* (Anne Frank)
- *Night* (Elie Wiesel)

- *Survival in Auschwitz* (Primo Levi)
- *Man's Search for Meaning* (Viktor Frankl)
- *The Book Thief* (Markus Zusak)
- *The Boy in the Striped Pajamas* (John Boyne)
- Poetry of Paul Celan
- Poetry of Nelly Sachs
- Poetry of Dan Pagis

Music:

- *Symphony of Sorrowful Songs* (Henryk Gorecki)
- *Quartet for the End of Time* (Olivier Messiaen)
- *Songs from the Theresienstadt Ghetto* (Various Artists)
- *A Survivor from Warsaw* (Arnold Schoenberg)
- Symphony No. 13 "Babi Yar" (Dmitri Shostakovich)
- *War Requiem* (Benjamin Britten)
- "Dance Me to the End of Love" (Leonard Cohen)

Film:

- *Schindler's List* (1993)
- *Night and Fog* (Nuit et Brouillard) (1956)
- *The Shop on Main Street* (Obchod na korze) (1965)
- *The Pianist* (2002) (The score for this movie features Chopin's Andante Spianato, which was the prelude's featured work of art!)

After taking in the work of art you chose, what spiritual or philosophical questions did it raise for you? Write them down without holding back.

Now, imagine the person or people writing or depicted in these works of art. Close your eyes and consider Ruth Duckworth's image of life as a unity, that all things are one giant lump of clay. Place your hand on your heart and connect for a moment with all those who have suffered across time. What are you wondering now?

Turn your questions into a prayer and read it aloud.

Chapter 8

Let Go, Let Go, Let Go
Arvo Pärt, "Spiegel im Spiegel" (1978)

If I speak in the tongues of humans and of angels but do not have love, I am a noisy gong or a clanging cymbal. And if I have prophetic powers and understand all mysteries and all knowledge and if I have all faith so as to remove mountains but do not have love, I am nothing. If I give away all my possessions and if I hand over my body so that I may boast but do not have love, I gain nothing.

Love is patient; love is kind; love is not envious or boastful or arrogant or rude. It does not insist on its own way; it is not irritable; it keeps no record of wrongs; it does not rejoice in wrongdoing but rejoices in the truth. It bears all things, believes all things, hopes all things, endures all things.

Love never ends. But as for prophecies, they will come to an end; as for tongues, they will cease; as for knowledge, it will come to an end. For we know only in part, and we prophesy only in part, but when the complete comes, the partial will come to an end. When I was a child, I spoke like a child, I thought like a child, I reasoned like a child. When I became an adult, I put an end to childish ways. For now we see only a reflection, as in a mirror, but then we will see face to face. Now I know only in part; then I will know fully, even as I have been fully known. And now faith, hope, and love remain, these three, and the greatest of these is love.

—1 Corinthians 13:1–13

There are many ways to begin this story.

I could start with how I was already in labor when I went in for my induction, forty-one weeks plus two days pregnant, well past full term.

I could tell you how I watched 2 a.m. come and go the night before, that we snapped a selfie in the driveway before we left for the hospital, my eyebrows raised as if I was thinking, *Well! Let's see how this goes!*

I could start by reassuring you that what happened to me that day ended with all of us healthy and thriving.

But where I want to begin is just before the darkness closed my eyes, before the world went away for a moment, before I woke up with a newborn. I want to tell you about how the best day of my life was also the worst day. I want to tell you that on the day I met my son, I also met my Maker.

Beyond the Pain

I never knew that in between the waves, in the lull right before another contraction comes, there is an awful dread, a quivering stillness, a foreboding, like being at the bottom of the roller-coaster, beginning the climb again, knowing another terrifying fall is coming.

I had labored for almost twenty hours unmedicated, thrashed around by those waves of pain, and I was nearing the edge—of what, I didn't know.

My husband, Edwin, had put on my "birth-day" playlist, like he promised he would, but up until that point, it was a mere murmur. As another painful contraction ended, I fell back and waited for the by-then-familiar despair to return, but instead, the shimmering arpeggios of Arvo Pärt's "Spiegel im Spiegel" came on, and I felt the warmth of the violin melody envelop me, the baseline pulsing like a heartbeat. Before I'd had any medication for the pain, with one hand seizing my husband's and the other gripped tightly to the metal bar of my hospital bed, all of a sudden, amid the searing burning of my body turning itself inside out, I felt it: euphoria.

I can say it no other way: I felt God's love enter the room.

Death Grip

When my daughter was born, almost four years earlier, Love had felt so far away. After the non-emergency C-section, when they sewed my abdomen back together and tucked us all away in the sterile, eerie nest of a hospital room, it was past midnight. Eva, a couple of hours old, lay in the plastic bassinet between my husband and me, her thick, dark hair covered by a pink hospital hat, her chest rising and falling so effortlessly. By some miracle, both she and her father were sound asleep. As exhausted as I was, peace did not visit me. I tried to breathe, but my hands shook, my IV throbbed. I prayed with gratitude that she was OK, that *we* were OK, but the tears fell warm against my swollen, pink cheeks and into my hair.

How could I rest?
Who would protect her?

From the first day of my daughter's life, from the first day of my life as a mother, I could sum up my parenting style in one word: vigilance.

I watched other moms in my breastfeeding support groups and, as Eva grew, in Mommy-and-Me Music and then group cello classes—they all seemed to know something I didn't. They were enjoying their children. I would watch them in the wild with wonder. How did they do this motherhood thing so effortlessly? They didn't seem to be staying up late obsessively watching their child breathe on the monitor, at least not that I knew. They weren't rehearsing everything that could go wrong.

When they closed their eyes, they saw the inside of their eyelids instead of the car careening off the road or the bookshelf falling on top of a tiny torso.

I sought support for postpartum anxiety, and while therapy helped, the disruptive thoughts, the constant need to monitor her, the dread about life in general, never left me. *This is what love does to us*, I remember thinking. Other parents seemed to be enjoying this parenthood dinner cruise while I had a death grip on the ship's railing, sure there was a storm coming.

A New-Old Lesson

A week or so before we were to meet the new baby, Eva's cello teacher, Mrs. Haley, was kneeling in front of this soon-to-be big sister, holding her hands, shaking them gently. She explained to my three-and-a-half-year-old a principle I knew well. Playing the cello, like playing any instrument, was about balanced pressure and release. "We 'chomp' the fingers on the strings," Mrs. Haley said. "We press down but don't grip. Mr. Thumb is the anchor. He stays relaxed." I watched her demonstrate. Her arms looked as graceful as a ballerina's, and Eva's eyes widened with joy.

Mrs. Haley would set up Eva's bow hand, place it perfectly on the string, and check to see if Mr. Thumb was too tight. Over and over, Eva would migrate back to that death grip on both bow and fingerboard, and over and over, Mrs. Haley would grab her hands, shake them gently, and say, "Let go a little for me."

By the time I had become a parent, I had sat through thousands of hours of music lessons. On that day, my lungs crammed up into my collar bone, my hands swollen, my oboe packed neatly and preemptively away for maternity leave, I heard something with fresh ears. I was beginning to see that all of music, all of parenting—all of life—could be summed up in this one invitation: "Let go a little for me."

We hold on too tightly because we think this is what love is. Fear of death grips us. It keeps us from enjoying our lives, from pulling the sound out of the instrument with any facility. Gripping tires us more quickly. Vigilance gives us a certain nervous energy that is helpful until our teeth crack from grinding and our shoulder muscles feel full of rocks, until a trip to the beach or the pool throws us over the edge. We get short-tempered, even angry. Bitterness steals the sweetness of each moment, and just like a cello or an oboe gripped too tightly, our children screech and squeal. Eventually, we realize our love has become pressurized; we've held them with this death grip, and ironically, our attempt to keep them safe has us on track to crush them—and ourselves—in the process.

Looking back, I see maybe God was trying to teach me this lesson before the new baby was born. In my condition, inviting another child into the mix was like pouring water on an anxiety grease fire. As I got closer and closer to the birth of my son, I felt my grip tightening—on Eva, on my birth plan, on our whole life.

When Love appeared to me in labor that day, it did not say "Let go a little," as Mrs. Haley did. I doubt I would have heard that message above the noise of my own fear. No, when this spiritual wave struck—larger than any wall of pain that threatened to drown me, mightier than any riptide I'd feared would sweep my child away, stronger than what I thought human beings could withstand—I had no other choice but to fully and completely surrender. It took me under. It wasn't so much a letting go but an involuntary emptying, a forfeit, both terrifying and exquisitely beautiful. With each breath, with each heartbeat, with each chord of the piano and the violin in harmony, I felt God whisper, *Let go, let go, let go.*

Ecstasy

Months and years later, when I went searching for words for what I'd experienced, I read that medieval mystics and others with spiritual visions often described it as a sense of "knowing." They may or may not have heard God's voice or seen God, per se, but they somehow knew God was there. My "knowing" felt like I had drawn near to the source of light itself. I was enveloped by an incandescence almost brighter than I could bear.

I read the word *ecstasy* in the writings of Catherine of Siena, Hildegard von Bingen, and Teresa of Avila and blushed. But that was it: a pleasure so pure and perfect that even attempting to describe it with limited, human words dimmed its light.

When I asked him about it later, Edwin told me he felt a change, too, in my face, in my body. Amid the grimaces of pain, there was a radiance, a joy, in my eyes.

As Edwin held me, as God held us, as my baby's heartbeat on the monitor fell in sync with the piano, as the music swelled and released, as I surrendered to the pain and joy of God's nearness, I began to cry and laugh at the same time.

I "saw" my daughter Eva, not a true visual expression of her, but a vision of her in my mind—she was headed off to college. She was leaving us. She was so beautiful, so precious, so grown. Imagine that deep joy you feel when you are so proud of someone, when you're so grateful to have loved them, to have known them, and as you watch them slip away, you know that it is right for them to go, but the pain and gratitude exist in equal measure. It was suddenly pure grace to be alive, to get to love her. I saw that to let her go was to love the Light that was the source of the brightness in her eyes, that was, miraculously, right there for me to bask in.

God came to me in childbirth to tell me that the rhythm of life is *let go, let go, let go.*

A couple of hours after the euphoric vision, after all that laboring, fully dilated, I pushed once more. My blood pressure spiked. My body seized. My son's heart rate decelerated. My world went dark. They took us both away.

A Holy Longing

Many years later, I'm still unraveling what this vision meant. Was it a gift of nearness before the darkness closed in? Was it to prepare me for all the things I would have to let go of in parenting, in life? Was it a warning that my anxiety was at odds with God's plan for my life? Maybe. Yes, probably.

All I know is that I got a taste of what the nearness of God feels like, which, in and of itself, was so overwhelmingly beautiful that I was tempted to pray for it to stop.

What I found most exquisite about it was how it wasn't a saccharine sweet lowercase love or a tirade of simplistic platitudes or even skin-deep, pain-free delight. It wasn't cheap or shallow, like so much of the pleasure we settle for in this life. It was a deep resonance, a vibration that set all music ringing, some truer joy that held grief and gratitude, pain and pleasure side by side.

Why would God show me Eva going to college, of all the possible visions? This is my best guess, here in the land of the living, years later: The circle of creation is made complete in the letting go of everything we love, in giving it back to the Source from which it came.

I've learned that when we are asked to let go, we aren't asked to deny our deepest longings, to forsake our love of all we cling to. No, by God's grace, when we let go, our longing is realized, seen, made holy.

Our children are not ours. The instruments or passions we hold so tightly to, these things we make, creations we cling to with death's grip—they are immortal. Death has no power to hold them, and neither do we. What I realized that day in labor, what music had been teaching me all along, was that this is good news. Life is a long letting go. Parenting is a letting go. Cello, oboe, music, art, and loving anything on earth are just one long exercise in letting go.

The Power of Art

"Spiegel im Spiegel" translates to "Mirror in a Mirror." It was written in a special minimalist technique called Tintinnabuli. This sparse, bell-like style evoked for Arvo Pärt, an Estonian composer, a deep spiritual dialogue between himself and God. The piano begins by playing the arpeggiated chords, punctuated by the rhythm of resonant bass notes, grounding the listener in hypnotic, pulsating peace. The violin enters with long sustained notes, and as the bow moves up and down in a cyclical gesture, these patterns against each other are a seemingly infinite reflection, a mirror in a mirror, on and on, forever (well, for nine minutes or so).

Pärt himself is a recluse, staying largely hidden from public life even as he remains one of the most performed modern composers of our time. In the 1960s Soviet Union, he composed mostly secular music in a modernist style. Then in 1968, his sacred choral work, "Credo" ("I Believe") was censured by the communist government. He retreated into himself, and instead of looking forward to what was next for modern music, he looked back, studying Gregorian chant and early liturgical music of the Orthodox Church. He converted to Orthodox Christianity in 1972 at the age of thirty-seven. Six years later, he wrote "Mirror in a Mirror."

His conversion story is not one he speaks about publicly, but in hearing his music on the best/worst day of my life, those Atoms Responding to Transcendence transported me. It felt like I had entered a conversation the composer had been having with God already. In my most vulnerable moment, this music pulled me into the vortex of God's infinite love. This is the power of art: across continents and lifetimes, it's a door to another world left ajar by a reclusive composer, a gateway to a spiritual connection that found me at the most vulnerable moment of my life.

But our hands must be free to open it, to let the art move us. To answer love's call to walk through the door, we must first let go.

The Greatest of These

Perhaps this is why the apostle Paul writes, right after the most famous passage in the Bible on love (1 Corinthians 13), that all things will pass away, that what we see on this side of the veil is just a dim reflection. Even the dim reflection shimmers and whispers of True Love, and so we are tempted to take whatever slice of human joy we find in this life and turn the mirror toward it, replicating it for infinity, making the human things we love ultimate. Suddenly, the vision of our "perfect life" gets more distorted the more the dim, earthly image is reflected.

Eva's cello lessons are a perfect example. Exposing her to music at a young age, giving her the chance to learn and thrive, supporting her, setting boundaries around the discipline of practice—these are all good things. When I am not careful, I make her progress at cello mean something about me as a parent, as a musician.

When she plays out of tune (as all beginners do), I cringe inside. Not because it hurts my ears, but because—I'm ashamed to say—it feels like an affront to all *my* hard work. All the times I have been down on my knees before bedtime, pointing with her bow at all the ways she needs to change. If I let myself, I could become a tyrannical musical dictator, all in the name of love.

This might seem like a trivial example but imagine that dynamic playing out on a larger scale, when she's choosing a college, a mate, a job. I want so desperately for her to thrive, to be safe, to be "OK." Even as I write that, I realize what I truly mean is that I want to control the outcome of her life, control life itself. But if—when—I allow these goals to become ultimate, I give them the power to steal both our joy.

Through the simple purity of Pärt's "Spiegel im Spiegel," I realized I had been looking in the wrong mirror. God doesn't ask us to be patient or kind, to not boast or never fail, by our own strength or admirable moral character. This is the distortion of disordered love, confusing lovely things for Love itself. Instead, God invites us to let the reflection of our Maker's perfect love stretch into infinity, as slow and steady as the bow of Pärt's violin, however dimly we may see it now. On that day the music opened a portal to this more profound reality. The order and simplicity, the power and spirit in it, made me hear so clearly how the dissonance of my own life trapped me. It showed me the spacious freedom God offers.

As a young person, I made my own success and pursuit of perfection an idol. I still do at times; it's a constant temptation. (I wrote a whole book about it, in fact.) God's call to let go during labor helped me see that my hyper-vigilance as a parent was actually my way of transferring this burden onto my child. When I do not let my children explore and learn (which involves making lots of mistakes), when I hold so tightly to this image I've made of her, of her life, of *my* life, these fantasies of perfection become more and more distorted, until the enormous weight of my expectations crushes us all.

Right after Paul's exposition on what love is, he says that knowledge, prophesy, tongues—examples of divine gifts given on this side of heaven—will pass away. In other words, good as they are, they won't last; we can't keep them. That day in the hospital, Divine Love called me to let all my gifts go, to return them to God. I learned that day that this is how we love without the objects of our affection destroying us.

These Sticky People

Eli Edwin Estevez was born while I was asleep. Those first days of his life are a medicated blur. The heavy dose they gave me to protect my brain as part of the eclamptic seizure protocol made me a bystander to the new joy around me, the previously hi-def world muted and far away.

Still, through the haze of that long, swollen, painful recovery, I knew we were not alone. I remember watching Eva hold her tiny brother in that hospital room. Noting with surprise (and then recognition) that she suddenly looked so much older, reminiscent of that young woman I'd seen in my vision. I sighed. I cried. I let go.

Every day that I wake up in the same world with this boy is a blessing. Eli, even at almost four years old, loves to hold my hand, with his deep, mischievous eyes and wild mop, a double-crown cowlick in the back. I give thanks every time I run my hands through his crazy hair (Yet another thing I cannot control!).

I can't protect them from everything, not really. I can tend to their needs, I can stay close, and I will. But with each milestone, with each pair of shoes they outgrow, with each new stage, I let myself cry the tears of both frustration and joy, trying to let go and give them to God.

On the stressful days, this looks like whispering to myself in the car, *let go, let go, let go*. It looks like examining my sour moods, my short temper, my disappointment of unmet expectations, and doing the harder work of figuring out how to lead instead of just demanding control. It means letting Eva play out of tune and letting Eli run on the hardwood floors with socks, even though he will most definitely slip and fall. It means trusting these little sticky people—with their wild art projects and messy meals—to do things themselves, their way, in their time, whenever that's possible (and if it doesn't result in major harm). It means raising them in the way of Jesus, letting them become the people God made them to be; it means setting them free. It sounds so easy, but it is the greatest challenge of my life.

An even deeper blessing comes, though, when we realize that, through this letting go of those we love, we are set free, too.

God knows the ache of open hands. I believe God gives us free will to love God, for one, which requires the possibility that we will choose not to. In sending Jesus to us, in letting him go to live but also suffer and die, God revealed the ultimate expression of Divine Love. Our Maker showed us the way to freedom, the terrifying yet exquisite truth that love's deepest power lies in its vulnerability, its willingness to risk everything for the sake of another, even knowing the potential for rejection and pain.

We can let go of our loves, knowing God went first.

What Letting Go Does Not Mean

I'm getting a lot of practice at letting go these days as my little family of four and I are given—by God's grace—the precious gift of time. Time that we very easily might not have been given; time that many don't receive.

Life is a letting go, but it isn't a long one for everyone. Most births are not euphoric, to put it lightly. Not all pregnancies end in a healthy mother and child. You might be thinking that it's easy for me to talk about letting go when I woke up from that seizure, unlike many who don't, when I have both my healthy children within arm's reach, when many don't. I do not know the pain of a short let-go, but I do know that however long any of us has is never enough.

If this sharper pain is your story, I want to tell you that the God I encountered that day in the hospital wanted us to know that we can release our death grip because there is an Infinite Love that never lets us go. We do not stop being beloved when our dearest ones are pulled from us, if or when we fail them, if or when our bodies fail us.

In our brokenness, with wounds that aren't so easily sewn closed, we do not need a faith strong enough to grip God, to cling to promises and platitudes despite heart-rending pain—only a faith willing to open its hands. God's grip is strong enough.

Letting go does not mean forgetting. It doesn't mean denying our deepest longings or pretending like we don't care what happens to our children. Letting go means trusting more in the infinite goodness of the Creator of this world than we do in ourselves. It means giving back to God what was always God's, allowing our Maker to give it back to us in God's eternity.

Let Go a Little for Me

Creating is, by definition, then, a letting go. We pour a part of ourselves into a song, poem, or painting and release it into the world. We want to control the outcome of our creative efforts, but we can't, and this is terrifying. Sometimes, often, that release is the hardest part.

If creating is the most loving thing God does, then every act of creation since is also an act of love, whether it is a book, baby, or a meal. It's a process that requires patience and kindness with ourselves and with others. It requires dedication and vision, sweat and tears (of joy, frustration, or both). If our loves are to stay in the right order, it also calls for complete and total surrender to the source of Love—the only one who never fails, who always protects, always trusts, always hopes, always perseveres.

So, let go a little. Release the death grip you have on your life, for you are immortal, too. Let go of your perfect plan. There is something surprising and more real ahead. Let go of the need for your first draft to be great. It doesn't need to be great; it just needs to exist. Let go of your children. Believe it or not, God loves them even more than you do. Let go of the shame you've felt for what you did or failed to do. By God's grace, there is still time. Release the pressure behind your air out through the reed. Let your fingers on the fingerboard go, let the music vibrate wholly.

And by let go, I mean *let God.*

Let God make all that is broken in this world, in you, beautiful. This is our Great Artist's specialty.

Look to our Creator and see the infinite harmony of this Divine Love, however dimly for now, a mirror in a mirror. Listen for the whisper of this eternal song: *let go, let God, let go, Let God, let go . . .*

ARS NOVA

Let Art Be a Soundtrack

The last half of this exercise was inspired by Julia Cameron's *The Artist's Way.*

Find a work of art that represents letting go for you.

"Spiegel im Spiegel" by Arvo Pärt is obviously my favorite, but two other musical ideas from the Western classical canon could be Barber's "Adagio for Strings" Op.11 or Gorecki's Symphony No. 3, Op. 36, also known as *Symphony of Sorrowful Songs.* If you don't resonate with classical music, Stevie Nicks's "Landslide" is another favorite.

As you listen or view the work, bring all the things you may hold too tightly to mind: your loved ones, your work, your future, your past, your dreams, ways you've been hurt, ways you've hurt others, stories of shame that haunt you, the good things you make ultimate, resentments, worries, fears, hopes, etc.

With each person or thing you name, place your hands on your heart and say aloud, "God's got this."

As you say it, breathe in and out deeply. Move your hands from your heart into an open-palmed gesture, resting both hands on your thighs or a table in front of you.

For example:

Breathe in: "Eva and Eli," [hands on heart].
Breathe out: "God's got this," [extended open palms].
Let the music stir in you the nearness and grace of divine love.

Part III

Source

Placard Poetry

"Reading like an artist" means the placards in the stone corridors of the American Museum of Natural History, in the middle of New York City, sound like poetry.

"All living things communicate."
Not just bird call, whale song, mating dance—but watercolors, the string texture of a Mahler symphony, a soprano's melisma, a resonant metaphor—all of ART has a bioluminescence we see and recognize.

"In nature, nothing is wasted."
What if the poems in your journal, the perfectly worded pitches that go unopened, the manuscript in the drawer, are nitrogen in the ecosystem? Energy captured and life cycled. Rain that is all at once precipitation, evaporation, and heavy clouds, all art, as Madeleine L'Engle says, "feeds the lake." Every effort put forth, every bit of creative life released, enters a process that your strength did not set in motion.

"Light is not fully understood; it acts as both a particle and a wave."
This mysterious and ephemeral light that Rembrandt and J. M. W. Turner chased, the brightness we attempt to capture in our vibrato and verse, how fitting that it evades science, too.

"The human eye can see about six thousand stars in the night sky."
If life is synonymous with expression, art is not something we make but a way we say yes to living. The Maker of these hundreds of billions of trillions of stars (twenty-four zeros, the sign says) lives. This Source sings through prophets and holy books, through galaxies, sunsets, and songbirds.

And so, every story becomes a parable, each song a symphony. Creating is us seeking the source; it is us remembering how to walk on water, a telescope that lets us see beyond the observable universe. Art, like all of life, is not a timeline but a spiral, pulling us further up and deeper in.

"You are stardust."
Deep within the bedrock of creation, there lies this truth: Even science is poetry; communication is, after everything, communion.

In creation, our Source seeks us.

Chapter 9

The Particular and Universal Wisdom of Created Things

Christi Belcourt, Wisdom of the Universe (2014)

> Great paintings—people flock to see them, they draw crowds, they're reproduced endlessly on coffee mugs and mouse pads and anything-you-like . . . But—if a painting really works down in your heart and changes the way you see, and think, and feel, you don't think, "oh, I love this picture because it's universal. I love this painting because it speaks to all mankind." That's not the reason anyone loves a piece of art. It's a secret whisper from an alleyway. "Psst, you. Hey kid. Yes you. . . . An individual heart-shock. . . . Yours, yours. I was painted for you."
>
> —Donna Tartt, *The Goldfinch*

The River's Consolation

On the day we buried my grandmother, I woke up in a room with a river view—the Cuyahoga River in Akron, Ohio, a town I'd visited once or twice a year my entire life. The community my mother grew up in was named after this river, but my grandparents' home on Marcia Boulevard was in a newer development away from downtown, a turn-of-the-century bungalow with a screened-in porch they lived in all summer, a shady backyard garden that the deer loved, and a dry, clean basement. In the spare bedroom upstairs, she'd read the children's books in the best voices. When you called her name from across that house, she'd respond with a gentle and charming whistle, her way of saying she heard you, that she was there, that she was alright.

On this particular morning, as I yawned awake in my hotel room, I was painfully aware that she wasn't there at the dining room table doing a puzzle. Her body waited for us at the funeral home.

I stood and stretched, then gasped as I opened the thin hotel curtains and looked down.

Some rivers have banks that are dense with vegetation, lush foliage that makes the water seem alive with fertility. I imagine the Amazon like this. The life source of a whole rainforest pulsing like an artery. I saw the Mississippi in New Orleans once, as wide as a lake. Its muddy waters swirled steadily as the levees buoyed the river cruisers, the air so heavy with humidity it felt like swimming to walk.

But this river in Akron, the day we buried my Daba, looked like a wound: centuries worth of rock worn down into a steep rocky ravine that throbbed with pain. I craned my neck so hard to see it from our ninth-floor window; it seemed to run underneath the hotel itself. I told my sister, with whom I was sharing the room, that I was going for coffee, and moments later, I stood in the empty basement restaurant, its floor-to-ceiling windows offering a better view.

I felt as if I were standing at the bottom of a rock quarry, the water had carved such deep crevices into a city of concrete. Above me were the highway overpass, the factory smoke stacks, remnants of Akron's industrial age. Below it all, a rushing torrent of water, a deep riverbed like a funnel. The earth had broken open to reveal some ancient ache. As I stood along the banks that morning, the smudge-proof glass between me and the land, my grandmother's city above me, the water like magma falling over ice-age sediment, I added my tears to its flow.

I read in a brochure in the lobby that some say the Cuyahoga River was named after an Indigenous word meaning "crooked" because it dramatically changes course in Akron. It flows south from Cleveland and Lake Erie, but just past the Sheraton where I stood on the morning of my Daba's funeral, it makes a U-turn. This isn't a man-made phenomenon but a natural geological process set in motion by the last glacial retreat of the Ice Age.

I thought of the men and women of this land who were here before the European settlers. I thought of the wars fought and the treaties signed and likely broken. I thought of the fires that raged when my mother was in high school, pollution making the rapids themselves catch fire. I thought of my Daba shoveling snow that would melt and evaporate and rain back into this river. I thought of all the water that had run over these rocks. I thought about how it was somehow still running now, even though she was gone.

Like swearing an oath or pronouncing a blessing, I held my hand against the window. I felt the rumble of the river's strength against the glass.

In lieu of flowers, my Creator sent me a river. Her torrent, rocky and reckless, consoled me. She did not look away as I cried. Her roar whispered of the Creator's love. The river's message, a question ringing through the bright Ohio morning: *If the water could flow through so much, couldn't I? What if this permanent transience is life?*

The Wisdom of the Universe

I think what we love about nature, what makes us want to be reconciled with it, is the fact that some part of our DNA remembers that we, too, are a part of her.

The artwork of Christi Belcourt, an Indigenous visual artist and activist, speaks to the interconnectedness of all things. She says, "All species, the lands, the waters are one beating organism that pulses like a heart. We are all a part of a whole." There it was again.

In grief and in joy, we stand in front of the rivers and sunsets of our lives, feel the spring wind against our skin after a long winter, and it is the closest we can get to seeing our love, our pain, our hope on a grand scale. God's artwork speaks of an audacious, unapologetic, abundant, extravagant love—one that holds space for grief and pain—and we are part of it.

This large-scale love and its whispered wisdom are beautifully manifested in Christi Belcourt's *Wisdom of the Universe*. The towering, nine-by-six-foot canvas imitates traditional Métis beadwork against a dark background. It teems with life, depicting colorful plants, flowers, and animals, many of them endangered in the artist's native Ontario. In her artist's statement for the piece, Belcourt says, "The planet already contains all the wisdom of the universe, as do you and I."

The first time I saw the impossibly bright reds and blues of Belcourt's canvas, the lush and wild symmetry—which upon closer inspection is playfully disrupted here and there like nature itself—when I heard the questions it asks about abundance and potential loss of the plants and animals it depicts, I felt the artist's yearning in the glimmering roots. I sensed her broken heart for all she feared losing and had already lost. I'd heard the same urgent cry of beauty and brokenness, a deep calling to deep, from the rushing torrent in Akron.

That day by the river, the rapids spoke to me of the irrevocability—the cost *and* the beauty—of love. The time-worn chasm of rock, the persistence and strength of water for millennia, finding a way, it met my longing with powerful and particular questions that pierced my heart with wisdom. I saw my grief and pain reflected in jagged rock and raging rapids;

this integral part of an ecosystem carried a message just for me. Like Belcourt's tiny dots making up a complex and intricate image, one river in a landscape was greater than the sum of its parts.

The wisdom of creation is not so much a soliloquy or sermon, but a whispered question left hanging in the air; more discourse than proclamation, impossibly particular yet universal.

Painted for You

In Donna Tartt's Pulitzer Prize–winning novel *The Goldfinch*, we learn the story of Theo Decker, a young boy whose mother tragically dies in a bombing of the Metropolitan Museum of Art. Theo survives, and in the aftermath of the tragedy, he steals Carel Fabritius's painting *The Goldfinch*, a small Dutch masterpiece that becomes a constant, if turbulent, presence in his life thereafter.

At the end of the story, his friend (turned family) James "Hobie" Hobart says these wise words about the power of the painting, the power of art in general: "But—if a painting really works down in your heart and changes the way you see, and think, and feel, you don't think, 'oh, I love this picture because it's universal. I love this painting because it speaks to all mankind.' That's not the reason anyone loves a piece of art. It's a secret whisper from an alleyway. 'Psst, you. Hey kid. Yes you. . . . An individual heart-shock. . . . Yours, yours. I was painted for you.'"

We love our sunsets and rivers because they are, by very definition, part of the universe, yet they feel anything but universal. Suddenly, the sky on fire, the sun sinking into the sea, a cardinal crossing your path, these works of art are how God loves us, how our creator calls to us, whispers from an alleyway, asks us questions that we are invited to carry like a well-worn rock from the riverbed.

Art echoes the wisdom of the universe—it speaks of a love at once individual and omnipresent, an interconnected ecosystem like a sweeping tapestry of color, which when you look more closely, is crafted from thousands of tiny dots.

Art sings of these paradoxes. It invites you into a conversation; its questions whisper into your deepest places of pain, and it calls you gently toward healing, a new understanding that stirs the pond; it is part of a whole but somehow created *just for you.*

From the Universal to Yours

As a child, I saw or sensed what Richard Rohr calls "the Universal Christ" everywhere in nature. I felt a kindredness with the authors of the Hebrew Scriptures, who personified creation: "The heavens are telling the glory of God, and the firmament proclaims his handiwork" (Psalm 19:1). "Let the floods clap their hands; let the hills sing together for joy" (Psalm 98:8) The writers of these ancient holy texts, those who saw the rivers and mountains multiple millennia ago, they stood on the same planet as I do, on the fertile banks and the rolling hills where they sensed both the power and the pain of this place, the life in the dust that humans were formed of, the love of the One who created it.

Summer in South Carolina meant the gift of long twilight. One evening, I remember swinging alone on the church playground. My older siblings must have been inside the small annex building in Methodist Youth Fellowship; my parents were likely inside cleaning up Wednesday Night Church or talking with friends my father had known all his life from having grown up in this church. Wherever they were, I was blissfully alone with God. I relished the moments to sing quietly to myself on the playground, even though on this particular evening, I was starting to feel I was getting too old, as a soon-to-be fourth grader, for swings and slides.

I remember feeling God in the wind against my back with each pass of the creaky swing. I would go as high as I possibly could and then launch my body forward, sending my eight-year-old frame into the air. Even back then, I had this sense that God loved me; God watched me, like a mother at the window, as I attempted to fly. I felt my creator smiling. I felt God loving me in the blues and oranges of the South Carolina sunset; in the grass, I sensed the lifeforce of this planet, my home, and I was grateful that it gave me something soft to land on. The entire world felt like a gift, a playground, from one who delighted in me.

Fast forward thirty years to another swing set, myself the mother at the window watching my children. Just a day or so before, I had learned of my grandmother's death.

It wasn't that I didn't still sense a universal goodness all around me. The sunsets alone that summer had been a balm for my weariness, a tenderness in the earth's new growth that season seemed to abound. I felt it in my precious, healthy children, creations that let out familiar squeals of delight, theirs in the Michigan twilight with speckled skies ablaze. But my childlike view of God was being drowned out right then by the cacophonous sounds of creation groaning (Romans 8:22). Nature seemed no longer like a loving mother watching at the window but more like some twisted death trap that threatened to destroy us all.

As I watched them play, I thought about all the things God had created that could hurt us. The yellow jackets. The snakes. The poison ivy. I felt tears right behind my eyes, and the temporary nature of all things seemed to be slapping me in the face. I thought of all that was left to do before I packed up and drove to Ohio for the funeral.

Daba's death was no surprise; she'd been declining. She was almost ninety years old. And yet, the pain was surprisingly sharp. No matter how hard I tried, no matter what nature would have me believe, death did not seem natural, certainly not good. It felt like she was being ripped from us. I didn't know how to explain it to my children, who were five and two. I didn't know how to explain it to myself, either. The loss was too great.

Then my faith became particular again.

A thought flew across my consciousness like a firefly, glowing for a second and then disappearing. As I watched Eva attempt to fly from our swings, just like me all those years before, my mind was halfway to Ohio, ready to stand with my mother as she buried hers. I let the tears run down my face. In that moment, Christ—Creator turned creation—whispered across the alleyway, like Theo's great painting, working his way so far down into my heart:

Didn't I have a mother, too?

I believed again, like a child.

The sky sang out, *yours, yours, I was painted for you.*

God's all-powerful grace pulls the threads of the universe together, and in Christ—a flesh-and-blood human with a mother whom he loved and lost—in him, a universal God is a particular God. Not "god" among many, but *this* specific God, in Jesus Christ.

Whispered Wisdom

What did Jesus love more than questions? In the Gospels alone, he asked a recorded 307 questions and answered only three directly. Some questions he answered with more questions. His parables left listeners standing there, incredulous, mouths gaping open. Most questions he answered or began answering with his life.

> "Who do you say that I am?" (Matthew 16:15)
> "Why do you call me 'Lord, Lord,' and do not do what I tell you?" (Luke 6:46)
> "Where is your faith?" (Luke 8:25)
> "Do you want to be made well?" (John 5:6)

It seems our only choice is to follow him if we want to find out.

It is the humble question-askers, those patient and trusting enough to tolerate these impossible queries he left mostly unanswered—it is these *meek*, Jesus tells us, that will inherit the earth (Matthew 5:5).

What does it mean that we have a Creator who isn't always so interested in placating our desire for control or works righteousness by giving us answers or making specific generalized prescriptions? What does it mean that God would rather engage our minds, invite us into a holy discourse that, in my lived experience, makes faith take root, find fertile ground to grow?

Since those days of standing at windows, against the fragile glass of grief, I make it my practice now to listen for the questions from Jesus, whispered in nature.

Before a woolly bear caterpillar becomes an Isabella tiger moth, it creates a cryoprotectant tissue, surviving by literally freezing itself solid until spring, stopping its own heart, freezing its gut, and ceasing its blood from pumping.

When I learned of this mysterious creature, I heard Christ, the wisdom of the universe, whisper: *Are you so concerned with what the butterfly will look like that you are missing the strength and miracles offered you in the caterpillar stage?*

Walking amid the pines, the brown needles at my feet, I realized: evergreens, contrary to popular belief, do actually lose their leaves. I read that they usually do so while new growth is already coming in, so we don't notice the needles falling until after the fact. The evergreen goes through the same process as deciduous trees, but differently.

The whisper: *Do you look at your deciduous sisters and envy their color? What if I have a unique process for you? Will you accept the gift of release, to let go of all that you grip so tightly, in my time?*

Tides are caused by the gravitational forces exerted on the earth by the moon, and to a lesser extent, the sun. Today, oceanographers are able to predict the magnitude and time of tides for a given location for up to a year in advance.

As the waves beat against the boat, the tide rolls onto my ankles, wetting my leggings, Jesus asks, *What, besides me, has a pull on you?*

Bonsai trees don't have special seeds that make them miniature. Their pruning, conditioning, and planting stop their growth. If you put the sapling in a different environment, if you stop trimming it and let it grow freely outside, it can become the size of a full-grown oak tree.

When I have been asking, "Why can't I grow?" wisdom whispers, *Is this the right pot?*

The Amazon rainforest contains eighty thousand different plant species. Twenty-five percent of the world's medicines are derived from those plants, and 70 percent of all plants with anti-cancer fighting properties exist *only* in the Amazon rainforest.

All this time, I'd been busy believing I had to create my own goodness or contribution to society, but I never stopped to consider that I was more like a rainforest than a robot. The whisper: *What wisdom have I hidden within you to discover?*

The endangered creatures from Belcourt's painting, the Dwarf Lake Iris, the Eastern Prairie Fringed Orchid, the

Karner Blue butterfly, the Cerulean Warbler, and the Acadian Flycatcher—these are questions our Maker asks, too:

What gifts have I given you to help the world heal?

May Art Be an Echo

I often sense, standing in front of a river or in a museum face to face with a towering canvas of color, that everything I've ever loved about art—every goosebump, that tightness in my throat, the rush of mirth—the more I think about it, the more it feels like what I love about art is really what I love about God.

God seeks me through the sky. The "with-ness" and vulnerability in a self-portrait, the power of ancient glacial sediment to make rivers change directions, each tiny "bead" in Belcourt's canvas, so particular in a universal whole: What if God, as artist, loved creation into being, and what if this is how God is still loving us today?

Jesus, being the wisdom of the universe himself (1 Corinthians 1:24), "God's particularity," who was with me on that church swing set when I was eight, who stood with me by the mighty Cuyahoga—who goes with me now, who goes with you—let us never forget, my friends, he is Lord of nature and he has conquered death (Colossians 1:16–17).

Before he died, he told a crowd, "And I, when I am lifted up from the earth, will draw all people to myself" (John 12:32). *How?* We ask. *When? Why does this life still feel so hard?* In response, we get only more questions, but hidden within each one is the whispered universal answer, *Love, love, love.*

May we always have ears to hear the quiet queries of creation. Let art be a way you are drawn to him. Be meek enough to live the questions that sing of God's particular love for *you*, in Christ.

In the face of all the brokenness of this specific universe, which demands we hold the paradox of "right now and not yet," the permanent transience of every river and every life, may you sense Jesus like a mother, a true Mother of Nature, longing to gather us like her chicks (Luke 13:34). He is at work in creation and in me even now, bringing salvation (from the Latin *salve*, which means healing), making all things new right before our eyes, one canvas, one sunset, one caterpillar, at a time.

As an artist yourself, may you set about the work of healing the world, with God's help. To fight for all that is endangered, to steward this gift of God's abundant beauty.

Collaborate with all that is already in motion, joining the current, the flow of living water—but watch out, it has been known to change your path.

Add your voice to a chorus that's been ringing since our Maker first breathed this world into existence.

May each work of art be an echo of that first breath, a whisper of wisdom, for every listening heart.

ARS NOVA

Let Art Be for You

What work of art feels like it was created for you?

Find one either in the natural world or the formal work of a human artist.

Take a moment to reflect on what about it feels personal and particular for you in this moment.

Imagine there's an epigraph—a short quote or statement at the beginning that frames the entire work—or a dedication written personally by the artist to you.

What would it say? What does the creator of the work of art want you, the one for whom it was made, to know?

Chapter 10

The Gospel According to Bach

J. S. Bach, "Mache dich, mein Herze, rein" from St Matthew Passion (1727)

Mache dich, mein Herze, rein,
Ich will Jesum selbst begraben.
Denn er soll nunmehr in mir
Für und für
Seine süße Ruhe haben
Welt, geh aus, laß Jesum ein!

Make yourself pure, my heart,
I want to bury Jesus myself.
For from now on he shall have in me,
forever and ever,
his sweet rest.
World, get out, let Jesus in!

—Translation by Pamela Dellal,
courtesy Emmanuel Music Inc.

Create in me a pure heart, O God,
    and renew a steadfast spirit within me.
Do not cast me from your presence
    or take your Holy Spirit from me.
Restore to me the joy of your salvation
and grant me a willing spirit, to sustain me.

—Psalm 51:10–12 NIV

Growing up in small-town South Carolina, when I first began belting the Bible songs in kids' choir at Main Street United Methodist, we realized, much to everyone's surprise, I could sing. I loved the way music felt in my chest, the songs poured out so easily and unselfconsciously. As I grew, all I wanted to do was play the beautiful music that I heard in my head, to open the score and read it effortlessly, just as our church organist, Mrs. Kerry Hall, did. My parents got us all piano lessons, and I would sit in the formal family room at the piano for hours and make up songs. I'd found the oboe almost by accident when I had the band director as my homeroom teacher in sixth grade. He'd said my personality (determined, bright, if a bit quirky) would be perfect for this instrument (difficult, poignant, if a bit quirky). So in eighth grade, I decided to quit cheerleading and get serious about music. I joined the band. I was surprised that a girl from the middle of nowhere, who had never heard an orchestra live before, who could barely read music, who was born into a "sports family," had talent for this persnickety, mysterious woodwind that everyone thought was a clarinet.

But yet, early in my musical life, alone with myself, I heard this question chasing me like an unpaid toll, "Am I good enough?"

Fast forward through the decades of intense conservatory training, including a boarding school for the arts, a Fulbright fellowship to Germany, and a stint in the Ivy League, decades of outrunning that question, brought me to Juilliard, a place that has a way of making the most abundant riches of talent look like pennies.

I wasn't a stand-out star in the studio, and everybody knew that, including me. First, I was five to ten years older than everyone. As a doctoral student, I felt I should be ahead of the eighteen-year-olds who played circles around me. Plus, the program was a challenging mix of academically demanding coursework, led by a panel of Harvard graduates who expected us to be scholars, set against an equally intense, competitive music performance program that demanded at least four hours of practice per day, plus reed-making. Up until that point, I had managed to hold on to my joy of music, if by a thread. But in the Juilliard years, I sensed a crescendo from the ensemble of my fragile ego, fear of failure, and a seemingly ever-decreasing natural aptitude or talent. By my second year at Juilliard, things were beginning to fall apart in a cacophonous mess of self-loathing and shame.

That's when I received an invitation to audition for a very prestigious summer festival. It was an unadvertised search for one oboist to fill a coveted spot in a chamber music program, and winning meant you had "made it." Name a famous oboist in the US, and most have taken part in this young artist training program.

As I waited for my audition outside the large wooden doors in the Rose Building, in the middle of a city full of people more talented than I felt I would ever be, I sighed. I looked down at the scores in my hand, an aria from J. S. Bach's *St Matthew Passion*, "Mache dich, mein Herze, rein" on top. On the upper corner of the first page, I'd translated the text in my intermediate German: "Make yourself pure, my heart."

I had seen this text many times, "sung" the words in my head as I practiced for hours. Bach's setting is joyful yet pleading, with that perfect mixture of graceful lilt and heartfelt lyricism that only Bach could write. It comes near the end of, in my opinion, his best piece, the *St Matthew Passion*, an oratorio (a dramatic vocal work similar to an opera but without staging), which tells the story of Jesus's arrest and death. The text from the aria is not drawn from Scripture but inspired by it. It was written by one of Bach's most popular lyricists, Picander. "Mache dich, mein Herze, rein" or "Make yourself pure, my heart," comes right after the emotional climax of the passion story, right after Judas betrays Jesus. Bach's placement of the song there felt to me like he was saying: *Before we follow Jesus to the cross, we're going to need to fix our hearts.*

I looked down at my handwriting on my score. I read through my translation again. *Mache dich, mein Herze, rein: Make yourself pure, my heart.*

Pure? My heart felt more broken, scared, twisted, and turbulent than pure. For years, I'd thought that if I had just gotten into college for music, if I'd just won this or that audition, if I'd just landed one of the coveted spots in the Juilliard program, then I'd be satisfied—then I'd finally know that I was good enough. Yet, with each desire of my heart achieved, I looked up to find the bar moved higher and higher, always just out of reach. The more I accomplished, the less I enjoyed it. The loftier the stakes, the further I had to fall.

I realized that these auditions, these large and small judgments I was using to determine my mood, my value as a human person, were their own type of betrayal. My younger self had dreamed of this moment, of an invitation such as this, but I had abandoned her long ago, all in the name of winning.

As I stood at that doorway, waiting for the proctor to walk me in, I felt like I was teetering on the edge of the skyscraper's roof. I wasn't sure what would happen to my heart if I kept going like this, if I didn't win this audition, or if I did.

At that moment, I felt the urge to pray, something I had been avoiding. All I could muster was an invocation I'd read once, that Bach scribbled at the top of some of his scores, the letters JJ, for *Jesu Juva*.

As I waited in yet another hallway to be judged, I whispered, "Jesus help."

Stepping into the Story

One thing I didn't know when I started playing music seriously was that devoting yourself to an instrument would mean encountering many stories, becoming part of them. Playing Bach in this audition felt like hearing a long-loved tale from a dear friend. More than that, it was like a great painting came down off the museum wall, and I was able to step into it. Every atom was imprinted with the Creator's insignia. When you're first starting to learn scales and simple children's songs, you don't realize that one day, with enough practice, the score could become another world you inhabit, a place of retreat and discovery.

Some have called Bach the "fifth evangelist." (After Matthew, Mark, Luke and John.) His devotion was evident in his letters and other writings, also in the asides of his well-worn Bible, discovered relatively recently, in 1934, in the attic of a Lutheran pastor's home in Frankenmuth, Michigan. Bach wrote some of the most complex canons and fugues in existence, as well as truly transcendent cantatas that gave Scripture a new voice.

Like the composer, I had grown up a Christian. Music and faith had always gone together, and yet, somehow, especially in the New York years, my faith felt like an old story I was no longer interested in telling. The Scriptures I'd memorized as a child echoed emptily in the splintered cavern of my heart. As I climbed higher and higher, God felt further and further away.

But that day in Bach's world, everything glowed with Christ. The shadows of my shame were scattered.

When it was my turn, as I started to play for a faceless committee behind a flimsy white plastic panel, the notes of "Mache dich"—so complex that they required a meticulously designed breath map and a near-perfect reed—felt as if they were written for me. *Make yourself pure, my heart*, became my psalm, and in my striving—in spite of it—that day, Jesus heard my prayer. The long phrases were an exhale, an ebb and flow of some deep wave within me, emotional and harmoniously heartfelt, all of it, communion—under a control that was beyond me, beyond this realm.

In that wood-paneled, windowless room, like a friend desperate to have me healed by Jesus, Bach broke through the roof (Mark 2:1–12); the music dropped me right at Jesus's feet.

The Answer

I love how David's songbook, his prayer journal set to music: The Psalms, sits in the very center of the Bible, at its very heart. Growing up, some part of me was afraid that faith in Jesus was a purely intellectual exercise, like a stern teacher who commanded me to abandon all feelings and obey. David's Psalms brought home for me the beauty of a messy and musical faith, the wholeness of God's desire to love and satisfy our deepest inner longings and our most profound understanding, reasoning, and thinking.

I realize, looking back, that my quite literal translation of the aria text with the reflexive verb showed my cards a bit, spiritually. "Make yourself pure, my heart," taken at face value, might have us believe that we could heal our hearts ourselves, that by our own strength we could hold on to God and find purity through our own righteousness. I realize now that this is one reason why my faith faltered in those days, why I had such disdain for the Bible; I thought, like greatness as an oboist, true faith was only given to those with enough diligence or discipline, that to follow Jesus one must be endowed with talent and a propensity toward perfection. I thought that, like a seat in a prestigious chamber music festival, purity was achieved by a perfect performance.

That day in the audition, the Jesus I met there—the Jesus I danced with inside the world Bach painted for me—laughed, and sang to me the words of that hymn from my childhood, "Cast your deadly doing down."

"Make yourself pure, my heart," became an invitation from my Maker—not for me to be good enough, but to believe that through Jesus, *God* is good enough. What if this was what Bach meant when he called our hearts to make themselves pure? To be like David, to let God *create* in us a clean heart, to set our hearts again on pursuing God's?

The verb in verse 10 of Psalm 51, "Create in me a pure heart, O God," is the same verb used in Genesis 1, when God ordered the chaos, when creation began. Creating, then, means making something out of nothing, *ex nihilo*, but it also means renewal, transformation, sanctification, rebirth. The man after God's own heart humbly asks for a clean one, and God doesn't fix it, dust it off, or point out all the ways the man was wrong; God goes to work as an artist and *creates* a pure heart in him, in all of us, again and again.

As I played the most transcendent audition of my life, as Jesus and I danced to Bach's music, God created in me a pure heart. I let go of all the ways I had been trying to earn love. I put down my impulse to make myself perfect: I had to in order to let myself be led, to be drawn beyond perfection into wholeness.

This time, when I asked if I was good enough, I heard Jesus whisper, "I am."

Serve the Gift

One question I plan to ask when I get to the other side: Why are some of us more talented than others? Talent's very nature seems exclusive, the sense that some have the "kiss of God" and others don't. It's perplexing, at best, and completely devastating, at worst.

I know, as someone with a complicated relationship with that word, as a creative coach to artists at a variety of levels, that talent talk leaves even the most confident artists standing face to face with their human limits; fears of failure and success are equally paralyzing. Is the talent I've been given *enough*? Why did that person, the one who doesn't *deserve* it, get more? Will there be a day when the jig is up and the abilities I have been given run out? When jealousy and comparison rear their heads, we become petulant children, screaming of scarcity. If art is how God loves us, then does God love those who have the talent to win auditions more than those who don't?

But author Madeleine L'Engle, in her book *Walking on Water*, offers another perspective, shifting our focus from performance to collaboration: "If the work comes to the artist and says, 'Here I am, serve me,' then the job of the artist, great or small, is to serve. The amount of the artist's talent is not what it is about." She names this humble and selfless way of approaching art "Serving the Work," as in offering up our gifts. It means believing that any inspiration we find, any great idea, any talent we have, all are gifts from God. Not rewards or signs of special favor, but gifts freely given for us to use to create beauty in collaboration with the great Artist.

L'Engle reminds us that faith—like art, which she sees as one and the same—isn't another audition you win or lose. It is a relationship you cultivate, a conversation you have each moment of each day. That this is the work of our life: to serve the gifts, the work we have been given to do, and by transference, serve God.

Before that audition, I'd been looking at talent, or lack thereof, as proof that God loved me or didn't, that I was good enough to merit God's love or wasn't. My own ego and desire to achieve was so loud it made it impossible for me to listen to the work, to serve the gifts that I'd been given. Suddenly, I sensed that talent wasn't some tool to measure my belovedness, but an invitation to experience a freedom and purity I'd given up on long ago.

A God After Your Own Heart

We are eager to take the matter of purifying our hearts into our own hands, aren't we?

In Bible study, I learned that when the Scriptures use the word *heart*, it means more than one's emotions. The Hebrew word לב (transliterated as *lev*) is more a holistic inner landscape that encompasses our feelings, but also includes reason, intellect, conscience, and intention. So, when David, in Psalm 51 prays, "Create in me a pure heart, oh God, and restore a right spirit within me," and later "restore to me the joy of your salvation," he means, let my heart burn with love for you again, but also, help me remember with my heart, soul, and mind that the healing you bring is *joy*. Purity comes from healing, not the other way around.

It's easy to read Bach's aria text or Psalm 51:10 and write off the idea of purity as something obsolete for those living outside of Jewish law. In ancient Israel, the idea of ritual cleanliness meant being able to enter the Temple, to fully participate in God's work in the world, in community with others, reassured that the glory of God would not destroy you as you drew near. Purity was more than being without sin, cleaned up, and "fixed." It was living in alignment with reality, to know that God is the Master of the Universe, and we are God's. It is letting ourselves be healed; we cannot do that for ourselves.

Even if we aren't living within Jewish purity laws, we still long for a "right spirit," our joy to be returned to us. I sensed, even in my spiritual wandering, that it would take something drastic, like a pure heart, to get through life without being crushed by the weight of my own ambitions.

The anxiety and temptation to idolatry that can creep in with our fears about talent—these are a heart issue. God meets us there to heal it.

As I sang through my oboe *Make yourself pure, my heart*, I realized that creative endeavors are not how we achieve and excel, nor prove our value as a person, but a place where we can be made clean. As an artist, God's sanctification power is, first and foremost, creative.

When we serve the gift, we live inside the score of a Creator who is not after our performance, but our heart.

Getting Out of the Way

That day was the only day in nearly thirty years of playing the oboe where the music I heard in my head paled in comparison to what we heard in the room. Usually, it's the opposite.

The Bach ended, and the Mozart, Strauss, and Barber that followed shimmered with a beauty I cannot, to this day, explain. I've shared throughout this book many of these moments of transcendence, the different feelings of Ultimate Reality, Jesus Himself, Holy Spirit, a still small voice, and others that found me through art—but that day, through the music of a composer who had known what it was to follow Jesus, who had served the gift, I was delivered into the heart of God, and there my Creator created me a new, pure one.

The audition ended, and I stood on holy ground. As I packed up in the hallway to leave, I remember the proctor—who'd led me into the room, who'd been there next to me while I played—stood by, speechless. I looked up and noticed tears in his eyes. And in mine. I shook his hand and thanked him, and we both just waited in that moment, smiling.

I finally understood what L'Engle means when she writes, "When the artist is truly the servant of the work, the work is better than the artist; Shakespeare knew how to listen to his work, and so he often wrote better than he could write . . . When the work takes over, then the artist is enabled to get out of the way, not to interfere." I had finally stopped obsessing over my own talent and focused instead on the music, on the song my Creator had written, through Bach's hands, just for me. I had finally gotten out of the way, serving the work instead of expecting it to serve me.

Outside, I stopped, frozen in the Manhattan evening, suspended on the pedestrian bridge over 65th street, the city lights haloed as I let the tears of joy fall. Bach was a bridge, and I wanted to walk back to Jesus. I found myself praying, whether or not I'd won the audition, that God would never let me forget this moment.

Lay Your Deadly Doing Down

In Bach's Bible, there are numerous handwritten notes in the margins. One such annotation occurs near 2 Chronicles 5:13. This Scripture tells the story of when God brings the Israelites together and commands them to bring the ark of the covenant, the representation of God in their midst, into Solomon's Temple, newly built/constructed. They begin to dedicate the temple with music:

> It was the duty of the trumpeters and singers together to make themselves heard in unison in praise and thanksgiving to the Lord, and when the song was raised, with trumpets and cymbals and other musical instruments, in praise to the Lord, "For he is good, for his steadfast love endures forever," the house, the house of the Lord, was filled with a cloud, so that the priests could not stand to minister because of the cloud, for the glory of the Lord filled the house of God. (2 Chronicles 5:13–14)

Alongside this passage, in the margin, Bach wrote, "Where there is devotional music, God is always present with his grace."

Most don't know that, in his lifetime, Bach struggled to find recognition and stability in his career. He was always highly respected as an organist and keyboard player in Germany and in parts of the larger musical community in Europe, but his compositions were deemed by many to be too complex, too difficult. He was passed over for many jobs; he lost many auditions. He died a respected organist, but it wasn't until a century later, when Felix Mendelssohn was given a score of Bach's *St Matthew Passion* by his Jewish grandmother and presented it with the Gewandhaus Orchestra in Leipzig, that Bach's music found its audience. That performance began the Bach renaissance that still continues to this day, as new manuscripts and writings resurface even in our time.

Now Bach is widely known as one of the top composers of all time, but in his day, he could have easily felt he had no talent at all if he were looking to the world for validation. Plus, his life was immensely difficult, full of rejections and a lack of money, a myriad of health problems, including eventual blindness from a botched surgery. Out of his twenty children, only ten lived to adulthood. Yet, his music was a faithful witness; he served the gift. All the talent he'd been given was not for his own glory and accolade but a result of his pursuit of God.

In the story of the Temple dedication, the cloud is so all-consuming that "the priests could not perform their service . . . for the glory of the Lord filled the Temple of God." This confirms something I learned in my audition: God wants to dance with us, to sing to us, to tear down the false gods of our egos with a cloud of divine presence so immense that it makes our "doing" obsolete. The swell I felt in my heart as I sang in church as a child, the joy of each oboe exhale in that transcendent audition, this was, of course, the grace of God. The Giver of Breath wants every part of us restored to joy, not just our heart or feelings, but also our intellect, our talent, our hard work, our winning, and our losing. Every note in life's aria becomes a word from God, a life our Maker is creating, transforming even now.

World, Get Out

A week or so after my audition, when I walked in a few minutes late to our oboe studio class, I saw everyone hugging and shaking hands with a colleague who'd just learned that she'd been chosen for the festival.

It stung, to be sure, that after such a mystical experience, I wasn't given the satisfaction of being named the winner. The months and years that followed this rejection continued to purify something in me. With a new heart, I was starting to understand what Bach said in the last line of the aria, "World, get out; Jesus, come in." When we truly serve the gift, our offerings become a communion with our Maker, and if or when the world doesn't recognize, applaud, or praise us for them, it isn't a verdict of our worthiness or a judgment of our value. It's irrelevant to a heart set on God. When we serve the gift, through sacred or secular art, in windowless rooms or ancient temples, no matter how good we are, no matter whether we win or lose, God is present with grace.

I will never create anything that compares to Bach's music, but what I learned from living inside his heavenly compositions—what I understand from knowing him through his complex and intricate melodies, his surprising and profound harmonizations, his lesson that day in the best audition I'd ever played, that I didn't win—is that talent is not a tool but a vessel. It is God creating us, finding within the impurities of our hearts the raw material of something greater than we can see in this lifetime. Talent is a gift God gives us of divine presence and grace. What if that is more than enough?

What I Was Really After

We can add "talent" to the list of things on this side of heaven that I do not fully understand. I still carry with me many questions. I do not understand God's ways; "Such knowledge is too wonderful for me, too lofty for me to attain," as David says in Psalm 139. Since I experienced the grace of God in that audition, I realized that my heart would never be satisfied with earthly accolades anyway.

After the initial shock of my colleague's winning wore off, all I wanted to do was practice Bach. It was communion with God that I was after now. The joy of my salvation, of my inborn creativity, is restored again and again as I serve the gifts I have been given. To devote myself to this music was not about winning or judgment; it became a path back to Jesus himself.

As L'Engle reminds us, "Getting out of the way and listening is not something that comes easily, either in art or in prayer." It's easy to allow our egos to loom so large that our hunger is all we can hear. Then, we miss knowing and being known.

I realized that day of the audition that I hadn't really been *listening* to Scripture for a long time, maybe ever. The Gospel According to Bach was about all I could bear back then. If our stories are how we know and are known, then God's written word, as complex and complicated as a Bach cantata, might be an invitation to know Jesus's heart. Indeed, this is why Jesus quoted Scriptures so often: he knew that singing the psalms, telling and retelling the stories, brings us to the very heart of God, where there is healing, where there is joy. If it was possible, I thought, through practice and devotion, to inhabit the world of Bach, then maybe I could try again with Scripture. Maybe I could learn to quiet the clamor of fear and insecurity enough to allow God to speak to me through these stories.

There comes a point in every relationship where you have loved someone so deeply and for so long that you know all their stories already. I've heard my father tell the story of how he met my mother so many times that I could repeat it verbatim, for example. The way he tells it reveals what matters to him, what he most values—the joy and miracle of finding a person in a bar in coastal South Carolina that you'd like to spend the rest of your life with.

When shared, our stories become a creative offering through which we are known. Reading the Bible this way—with a heart seeking to encounter the heart of God—has changed everything for me. I read it now, looking for what God values, what matters to God; to know our Creator's stories is to know God, to hear the music of the very Giver of Breath's voice above the noise of my own ego, to know God by heart.

Prodigal

God has promised to provide for us what we need; like manna in the desert (Exodus 16), there is no deficit of ideas, gigs, baselines, metaphors, and we can trust that there will be enough. This doesn't mean we will always win. It doesn't mean our lives will be easy. It doesn't mean we will be loved and praised and prosperous all our lives; we have Bach and Jesus as proof that isn't true. But we can trust that God's plan is better than ours, that the arc of the universe is long and full of art.

If you are tempted to believe that being an artist is frivolous, that we are only useful to God when we perform acts of dramatic impact, that we are only valuable when we earn the praise of the world, remember that we are created in God's image to create. Remember that God creates clean hearts, that God orders the chaos of creation, that God's artistry is synonymous with God's love.

Now, I know that when something clicks, when something happens on the stage or in the audition room that feels transcendent, when my chest swells, all these years, all along, it was the cloud of God's presence, just as God promised, loving me, healing me. By the light of this realization, my obsession with talent feels petulant, limited. Like the elder brother in Jesus's Prodigal Son parable (Luke 15:11–32), I see myself complaining that God loves others more, when God has already given me everything.

We risk missing God, present with divine grace, when we focus on the merits of our own performance.

I won't pretend I never struggle with doubts of my own worth or talent. It did and still does hurt when I don't succeed, but it doesn't have the power to destroy me anymore. This is no small miracle. I know now that when I feel the very human desire to be great, it is an invitation to step aside, not by accepting mediocrity or giving up, but by serving the gift—allowing *God's* greatness to come through me, trusting the Spirit will lead me, like a partner on the dance floor, through each note I play.

This is my prayer for you, and for me. That if—when—we find ourselves asking if we're good enough, we will trust our Maker when God answers, "I AM." That we will sing along to the psalmist's refrain, "his love endures forever," and feel it in our bones. That we will let God create in us a new heart, transcending our limited earthly talents into a temple of grace. That we will realize that every time we enter the audition room or open our notebook or arrive at the easel, we step into God's story of healing love. Before we play a note or write a word, what if, this audition committee of one is already delighting in what we create?

Create in me a clean heart, O God. Amen.

ARS NOVA

Let Art Heal Your Heart

Cellist Pablo Casals, the artist credited with popularizing the Bach cello suites when he found an old copy of the manuscript in a music store in Spain, said once, "For the past eighty years I have started each day in the same manner. I go to the piano, and I play two preludes and fugues of Bach. I cannot think of doing otherwise. It is a sort of benediction on the house."

More than our houses need a blessing, don't they?

Find a recording or the score to the music of J. S. Bach, any instrument or genre—vocal, instrumental, with text or without—and find a quiet place to listen or play alone.

Take a moment to name in the silence of your heart all that longs to be healed.

Let your body move to the music in whatever way feels natural to you, tap your foot, breathe in and out, let Bach bless you as his music speaks of God.

Interlude

Sunset Alert

> But perhaps God is strong enough to exult in monotony. It is possible that God says every morning, "Do it again" to the sun; and every evening, "Do it again" to the moon. It may not be automatic necessity that makes all daisies alike; it may be that God makes every daisy separately, but has never got tired of making them. It may be that He has the eternal appetite of infancy; for we have sinned and grown old, and our Father is younger than we.
>
> —G. K. Chesterton, *Orthodoxy*

In our house, we have a rule.

When someone yells, "Sunset Alert!" you push the pan off the hot eye, turn from where you kneel folding laundry, put down the toys, close your laptop. You rise from the solitary steam of your bubble bath, and you waddle to the uninsulated porch in a wet bathrobe.

I'm not sure how it started or who first uttered the words at top volume. I don't know how we became these wild, grateful, sky-watching people.

Dripping bubbles onto the vinyl flooring we'd hope would pass for hardwood, in this house where nothing ever seemed to stay fixed, as I observe my daisies turn toward what they call "The God Show," I realize this daily celestial bedtime routine is an invitation from my Creator to feel beloved, to add my voice to the chorus, as Chesterton says, of those young and strong enough to exult in the sometimes glorious, always miraculous, monotony of this precious gift called life.

A lavender, cotton candy sky will always be my favorite emergency.

Chapter 11

Portfolio Life

Billy Collins, "Introduction to Poetry" (1988)

Metaphor is the only language we have to speak of God.

—Pete Holmes

A time-worn, gilded frame with a photo from the last century sits on my desk. It was my grandmother's, collected from her belongings by my mother and given to me when she died. The photo features a sixteen-year-old me seated at a dusty piano circa 1999 at the Veranda Café. My grandmother (whom we called Daba) may have come to visit from Ohio one of the nights I was playing, or my mother may have mailed her the photo after the fact. My first official "gig," as a high school freshman, was providing background music there, a small restaurant just off the town square inside a department store in my hometown in rural South Carolina.

In the photo, I'm sitting at the rickety brown baby grand in a long black velvet dress—my school choir concert uniform, if my memory serves me. My hair and shoes date the image a bit, but other than that, there's a timelessness to it. I recognize the familiar light in my eyes, the seriousness behind them. On the outside of the frame, Daba had scotch-taped a portion of another photo, the sign outside the restaurant: "The Veranda Café presents . . . Meri Hite at the piano, Saturday, 5 pm–8 pm."

The main things I remember from this gig were twofold: a restaurant patron asked me to play more softly so he could "hear himself think," and the fact that this review was made only slightly less brutal by the delicious twice-baked potato I got for free at 8:05. These details rush back as I hold the frame, the feeling of the piano's squeaky pedal against my high-heeled sandals, the thrill of having a real "gig," but also a general and overwhelming sense of insecurity and inferiority.

Back then, I mostly played piano by ear. For as much grace as Mrs. Grace Utsey, my childhood piano teacher, had, she could not teach me how to read music. I constantly resisted. I would beg her to just play the song once, so, back home, I could plunk it out on my own; I'd get there eventually by trial and error.

By age fifteen, I'd figured out chords to popular, easy-listening tunes and even written some sweet and melancholy (if completely derivative) pieces of my own. I played from the *Easy Book of Piano Classics*, with tunes of Beethoven, Debussy, and others stripped down and in simpler keys for less-experienced pianists. The only problem was the shameful fact that I wasn't playing the "real music." Even though I came from a family of non-musicians who wouldn't know the difference, even though no one ever once insinuated as much, the "fake book" made me a fraud in my own mind. Still, this parlay into music performance gave me hope. I looked forward to these evenings, feeling a little more grown up; I enjoyed being paid in two crisp $20 bills and in potatoes with Southern-style portions of butter, bacon, and cheese, all for doing something I enjoyed.

Recently, when I was tidying my desk—in lieu of writing—I noticed the picture frame's thickness. There seemed to be more photos behind the main one. I eagerly grabbed it and settled into my chair. If you've ever gone through the things of someone no longer living, you've felt this familiar thrill of energy, bracing yourself, hoping to find something new, something meaningful.

Maybe my Daba had a message for me.

The first thing I found when I slid the ancient glass back was my older brother's senior picture. My heart sank a little. In his rented tux and trademark smile, Thomas Erskine Hite, III (who we call Tombo, for short) looked shockingly like a young Brad Pitt. As much as I love him, I let out a gentle sigh of disdain for the seemingly effortless ease he had in his body when we were kids and even now. I was tempted to roll my eyes but decided Daba would likely disapprove of that behavior, which made me smile.

To my delight, behind my brother's picture, there were more photos. I turned over a photo of an infant, precariously propped up in a cream-colored bonnet and flower-smocked dress. It read, "Merideth, 5 months, April 1984." Then, another picture behind it that I had definitely never seen before. It was simply labeled "1999." There I was again, in all my young teen glory, Abercrombie-clad with wispy, unruly bangs, standing in my grandmother's foyer in the house on Ridgeview Boulevard. I'd brought my oboe with me to Ohio over Christmas and had been practicing. She snapped a photo of me awkwardly holding the assembled instrument and my massive portfolio of band music overflowing, smiling knowingly with my trademark awkward charm.

Part of me looked at these pictures in hopes of hearing a message from my grandmother. Another part of me was searching for something else: answers to questions I am still asking more than twenty-five years later.

Portfolio Overflow

Over breakfast at a café recently, my husband and I were discussing my schedule. In addition to my life as a musician and mother, I am balancing (though not well, frankly) an exciting writing life—speaking events, podcasting, and coaching, attempting to write another book while trying to make sure no one forgets about the first one. As the conductor of this beautiful, chaotic, two-ton locomotive, I smile through clenched teeth. Everything's fine. But deep down, I have felt the train speeding up and rattling a bit on the tracks for weeks (months?) now.

I shared my insecurity and confusion with my husband: What are the best ratios of activities in my creative life? Why do I do this to myself? I told him how, since the first book, I am starting to feel less and less like a musician who writes and more like a writer who occasionally plays music. I shared how interwoven my identities are with each of these aspects of my work and how leaning into all of them with my whole heart is impossible, yet I try and try and feel like I fail and fail. It is as if my life is some fully-composed song that, if I just try hard enough, I can figure out the notes and eventually get right.

People call this type of career—with different income streams, job titles, and roles—a "portfolio career." I like this name. The girl at the piano and the foyer holding her oboe would like this life, a chance to follow her multiple interests, to use energy toward many things she enjoys and make a living in a multifaceted, multi-passionate way. (And hey, sometimes there's even money for twice-baked potatoes!)

Yet, there is a psychological toll a portfolio career can take on an artist. While it is amazing to play in an orchestra one minute and tour as an author the next, moving from one intense, all-consuming work to another can be acutely stressful, not to mention logistically hectic and mentally draining.

I remember one evening last year when I'd agreed to an oboe gig with a local chamber music group I was eager to play with. I'd cleared with the personnel manager and the conductor before the services began that I'd be late for the second rehearsal because that evening was the first meeting of my online creative cluster that winter. Over five hundred people showed up to that meeting. I was astonished and overwhelmed, and so was my Zoom account. Some participants were locked out for the first ten minutes while we rushed to increase the subscription capacity in a panicked attempt. It all worked out (thanks, in part, to my lovely co-facilitators), and as I sent the participants to breakout rooms for the middle thirty-minute portion of the meeting, I came back to myself and realized that I then needed to drive to my gig, which I did with the laptop open in the passenger seat, so I could do the final portion of the meeting from my car in the parking lot and run right into rehearsal afterward.

Did I execute all those things? Did the internet hold and the traffic flow? Did I run into the hall where the rehearsal was and play exactly when I was supposed to? Yes, yes, and yes. Did I get a speeding ticket on the way home from all the adrenaline? Also, yes. I am ashamed to say, as a creative wellness coach, that this life, this "successful" portfolio career, as exhilarating as it can be, often feels unsustainable and terribly exhausting.

Maybe you're thinking, why would you do that to yourself? Turn down the gig! Prioritize! Say "no" more often! It isn't that simple. Besides the internal struggles of longing to maintain my identity as an oboist, something I had trained to do since I was fifteen, there are also the outer narratives and stigmas that keep me up at night.

Fake Book

Ask anyone what it's like to have a portfolio career, and they'll tell you about the impostor syndrome and fear of losing skill in one area, how we compensate by attempting to be better than perfect, by doing everything, and by being everywhere. I over-commit and over-deliver because I love what I do, but also because I'm afraid of losing something I can't quite name.

I am still outrunning that pesky lie I was taught as a student, that if you choose to be an oboist AND—a mother, a coach, a writer—then it must be because you aren't good enough to make a living solely as a musician. I'll show them, I mutter to myself as my eye twitches, and my stomach churns. There's also something more intrinsic at stake, something tied up with my identity that's even harder to dismiss.

As I sat at breakfast at forty-one years old, talking vulnerably with my husband, I realized that just like playing from a "fake book" at fifteen meant I wasn't a "real pianist," there is some part of me that still believes that doing more than one thing in my career makes me a fake at all of them. That even after all I am doing, it's not enough. I'm still asking some faceless gatekeeper if I deserve to be here. I'm still wondering: Who am I?

I finished my soliloquy and waited for him to speak.

Edwin let the silence linger and then said, "Well, you're not *techne*, that's for sure. You're *poiēma*."

Looking for the waitress to top me off—I'd put so much creamer in my coffee that it was now cold—I muttered, "What?" I glanced over to find Edwin smiling. This was one of the joys of having a seminary graduate as a husband: Your existential crisis questions get answered in Koine (Biblical) Greek.

Being a Poem

"For we are God's handiwork—masterpiece, craftsmanship, creative work—created in Christ Jesus to do good works, which God prepared in advance for us to do," he said, recalling the words by heart. Of course, I knew this verse from Paul's letter to the Ephesians (2:10 NIV); it was one of my favorite Scriptures. He explained, "The word for handiwork, masterpiece, etc. in Greek is *poiēma*, where we get the English word *poem*. Another word that the apostle Paul could have used to describe something made is *techne*, which is where we get the word *technology*. You aren't *techne*; you're *poiēma*. You're not God's technology; you're God's poem."

The words rang, resonant, a piano with the dampers up, a salve on some deep wound, vibrating with hope.

Our culture is exemplary at making tools. Got a problem? There's an app to fix it. We've got *techne* taken care of. When an old digital camera or cell phone starts slowing down, when you realize there's an opportunity for an upgrade, most of us discard them without a second thought. We get a new one—a faster, better, flashier one. Technology is only as valuable as what it can do, judged in comparison to the other technology around it.

Poems, on the other hand, are treasured topographies of existence, proof of life, existing for no other purpose than to speak some truth we couldn't otherwise say. We love poetry because of its potency, how it can tell a story in just a few lines, the mastery with which it is designed. The poet's care with choosing everything: the words at the end of the line break make the reader's eyes stop just a moment before dropping to the next; the syntax makes a rhythm—a pulse—and suddenly, language becomes music. The author reverently creates something deeper than our most languid sighs, something we learn and know by heart.

What if we believed we were made like that?

You upgrade and discard your old technology, but you would never throw out a poem because there's a newer, faster, better one. A poem is loved not because it's useful. It is loved, especially by the poet, because the poet made it, because it *is*, and is therefore beautiful.

And so it is with you and me. We are made for more than usefulness, efficiency, or productivity, more than portfolios of achievements and accolades that we are tempted to accept as love's counterfeit. God loves us only as an artist can: by creating things as beautiful and necessary as breathing. Hand-painting stars for us to see by, crafting not just one or two types of flowers, but innumerable, extravagant, creative joys that God calls good. God made the earth tilt on its axis just so that this planet could explode with life.

As Edwin reminded me over cold coffee and scrambled eggs, God relates to us as an artist to artwork—the greatest Artist, with quite a varied and prolific portfolio, mind you, working even our brokenness into a beautiful mosaic of meaning.

"Created in Christ Jesus to do good works, which God prepared in advance for us to do"—the Poet has already prepared the form of the epic of our lives; God has gone before us, and our Maker is still writing. We do not need to make our meaning, earn worthiness, like our life is some TV ad in which we must convince the world to buy what we are selling. It was all prepared in advance—we just get to delight in being a living poem, in exploring what beautiful meaning God has already hidden within us.

The Poet's Promise

After that breakfast epiphany, I decided to fall into some poetry myself. To see if God, the great Poet, would meet me there. When my eyes fell on Billy Collins's "Introduction to Poetry," I heard the message I was looking for inside that picture frame of my grandmother's, inside the poetry anthology; they both spoke to finding meaning in this beautiful mess.

I ask them to take a poem
and hold it up to the light
like a color slide

or press an ear against its hive.

I say drop a mouse into a poem
and watch him probe his way out,

or walk inside the poem's room
and feel the walls for a light switch.

I want them to waterski
across the surface of a poem
waving at the author's name on the shore.

But all they want to do
is tie the poem to a chair with rope
and torture a confession out of it.

They begin beating it with a hose
to find out what it really means.

Suddenly, the words on the page were not from some unknown speaker or Billy Collins but from my Poet, inviting me into a different search for meaning, as I read Billy Collins's "Introduction to Poetry," I was introduced again to the masterwork that is my life.

Are you tempted to tie your life to a chair and beat a confession out of it? Longing to know, for once and for all, who you are? Instead, what would it look like to hold your life up to the light like a color slide and enjoy its beauty?

When I do that, I see God's provision everywhere, the invisible presence in each picture in my grandmother's frame, in each gig, chapter, oboe reed, and book talk. God goes with me on every page of this portfolio career.

Pressing an ear against my life like a hive, as Collins strikingly puts it, means putting my striving down, trusting that everything I need is already in there, working, in spite of me. Like a beekeeper, I get to care for and cultivate the gifts God has given me, the good work in Christ that has already been prepared in advance for me to do, but the making of that delicious honey is not up to me. Taking every gig, every speaking engagement, constantly working beyond my limits in an effort to outrun my shame and insecurity—to earn my place at the creative table—is the metaphorical equivalent of me attempting to climb into the hive and do the work for those bees. I can be many things; I can trust that I belong, that I am not a fraud, because it isn't me who brings the growth or results or products; that is the job, the promise, of the Poet.

What if each experience, each risk I take in my work, were less like a confirmation hearing of my worthiness and more like watching a mouse work her way out of this predesigned, joy-filled experiment? What if I could trust that the answer to the question of how much oboe versus how much mothering versus how much writing will reveal itself as the experiment continues? What if, all along, what I thought was a rat race was actually an invitation to deeper curiosity, courage, and delight?

Walking into the rooms of my life, feeling the walls for the light switch, looks like trusting it has meaning already, that it is "right" already, "real" already. Stumbling around in the dark is a spiritual practice: believing the switch is there, having the courage to flip it on, allowing myself to see things differently than they may initially feel in the dark, trusting that whatever the light reveals will be good and so much more than good enough.

Waterskiing across the surface of my life's poem, waving at the author, means actually enjoying myself. Imagine that. Billy Collins's playfulness reminds us that not all poems need to be epic dramas of pain and suffering. Within the experience of riding life's waves, our creator delights in us, cheering us on with deep mirth and joy. Maybe sometimes I don't need to be so serious. When you're waterskiing, falling down is part of the experience. It isn't always pleasant—it can even hurt—but when you fall, you swim until it is time to get back up. The force that pulls you across the water is not your own strength. To waterski well, we have to surrender, to allow ourselves to skim across the surface, holding on to the rope and riding each wave that comes our way.

Meaning Is Not Something You Make

Do you find yourself working so hard, trying to prove your worthiness, running on dial-up internet like some piece of out-of-date technology? Do you wonder if you're doing enough or doing the right things the right way? As if life is a set of skill tests you're either passing or failing on a given day? Do you live in the scarcity and fear of having to do all the things, and perfectly?

The question "Who am I?" does not have a simple answer. How do you define a poem in a job title, a one-pager, or a two-hundred-word bio? You don't. Not only are we so much more complex and beautiful than that, but it's also missing the point. We don't have to define ourselves because we don't have to prove ourselves: We are already beloved, already made whole in Christ, and wholly known. As the comedian and author, Pete Holmes, says, "Metaphor is the only language we have to speak of God," because God is a poet, and we are the poem.

As creative as we are, our meaning is not something we make; there is no sheet music or fake book for that. It is something we can learn only by ear, by heart. It's something we discover, not by striving but by being.

Untie yourself from the chair. The meaning of your poem is already embedded within the very miracle of your existence from the first word, before you could ever earn it, even before someone propped you up in a bonnet as a baby for the church directory camera, even then. It is there in every snapshot through the years, the frame thick with all the *yous* you carry with you. The message from God is, in every age and stage and facet of your life's portfolio: "I love you, and you are mine."

What would believing you are God's masterpiece, believing you are God's *poiēma*, do for your courage, your self-esteem, your calendar, your general anxiety about the future? Will you let it make you bold enough to act, to go after that thing your heart longs for? Humble enough to trust that God has created good work for you to do and loves you too much to put the pen down now? Will you let it make you calm enough to stop cramming more into your overflowing schedule? Patient enough to let the right opportunities come to you in the fullness of time?

I had never thought to ask of my portfolio career—whose portfolio? Even if you have one income stream or art form you work in, consider the idea that we are all in the messy middle of a "portfolio career" in a deeper sense. It's called life. You are a *poiēma*, a prism—a multifaceted, profoundly unique expression of your Creator's joy. Perhaps a bit more complex than you'd like sometimes, but wonderfully made just the way you are, on purpose. Each experience is another line in the poem of our lives, overflowing with nuance and color, the masterwork revealing more about the Artist behind the portfolio than anything we could do or achieve.

When life feels unsustainable, when you are searching for meaning in the swells and ripples of these choppy waters, when you find yourself grasping for more instead of leaning back and enjoying the ride, take out the old photos, feel for the light switch, and hold them up to the light.

Don't just wave at the author's name on the shore; swim to your Maker, fall into God's arms, and let Christ love you like only the Artist can.

ARS NOVA

Let Art Speak of Your Poetry

Pull out a copy of your favorite poem.

Analyze it. What makes it so beloved? Below is a list of poetic devices that writers use to design poems. Circle or underline which ones are used in your favorite poem.

Alliteration
Assonance
Consonance

Onomatopoeia
Rhyme
Euphony
Cacophony
Repetition
Metaphor
Simile
Personification
Hyperbole
Imagery
Symbolism
Allusion
Irony
Paradox
Oxymoron
Synecdoche
Stanza
Line Break- End-stopped vs. Enjambment
Caesura
Meter
Verse Form
Meter
Rhyme scheme
Number of lines
Free Verse
Refrain
Inversion
Syntax

Now look at yourself like a poem. What makes you beloved by God? How did God design you especially? Look at your outward appearance, but also your character, sense of humor, likes and dislikes, even the things that you struggle to accept about yourself.

Turn what you wrote into a poem. If you are reticent about trying writing, I recommend borrowing the form of the Japanese three-line haiku. (True Japanese haiku is a little different, but I have found that borrowing the 5–7–5 syllable organization is a constraint that enables a creative invitation.)

Chapter 12

Creator Sets Free

Aurelius Prudentius/John Mason Neale, "Of the Father's Love Begotten" (1582)

Long ago, in the time before all the days, before the creation of all things, the one who is known as the Word was there face to face with the Great Spirit. This Word fully represents Creator and shows us who he is and what he is like. He has always been there from the beginning, for the Word and Creator are one and the same. Through the Word all things came into being, and not one thing exists that he did not create.

Creator's life shined out from the Word, giving light to all human beings. This is the true Light that comes to all the peoples of the world and shines on everyone. The Light shines into the darkness, and the darkness cannot overcome it or put it out.

Creator's Word became a flesh-and-blood human being and pitched his sacred tent among us, living as one of us.

Drawn from the Water (Moses) gave us our tribal laws, but the gift of great kindness and truth came from Creator Sets Free (Jesus), the Chosen One.

—The Gospel of John, 1:1–5, 14, 17,
First Nations Version: An Indigenous Translation of the New Testament

I had not planned on marrying a pastor. My comparatively serene days as a professional musician and college professor left me woefully underprepared for this chaotic (albeit joyful) life with my favorite Presbyterian.

What has surprised me most about this life is how simultaneously beautiful and harrowing it is to have a front-row seat to the human experience.

After nearly ten years at Edwin's side, I feel this phrase—the human experience—deep in my bones. I think about the couples he's wed, their babies he's baptized a year later. I think about the time when a call came during date night, and we turned from the restaurant toward the hospital. When the air in the room hung sterile and silent, save beeping machines, as Edwin asked the estranged family members to hold hands and pray. I think about the time my chest tightened as I sat in the back of the drafty church at the service for a young woman who died of an "overdose" (Edwin always says that word is a misnomer because there is no "correct dose" of heroin). I think about how he's appeared at retirement receptions, interventions, and even court on behalf of "parishioners." I use quotes because that word feels wrong. What do you call strangers you attempt to love with your life?

Most of us live these major transitions—the weddings and funerals, the births and deaths—only a few times with our own beloved ones. But it is the gift—and sometimes, simultaneously, the burden—of the pastor to approach these crossroads, the immediacy of the human experience, with bewildering regularity.

As I've watched "my person" withstand the whiplash of joy and pain, of malignancy and miracle, Frederick Buechner's oft-quoted words have become a gentle mantra: "Here is the world. Beautiful and terrible things will happen. Do not be afraid."

Today, they strike me as not unlike an angel's message, a proclamation to all who wait here outside of heaven, the brutal truth, a consolation, and a call to courage.

Of the Things That Are, That Have Been

One beautiful thing did happen one November. We were heading out to eat breakfast together, just the two of us, after Edwin had led a Veterans Day prayer service at an assisted living facility (on a morning off, mind you—the human experience does not observe Sabbath), when a church member grabbed him by the arm and said, "Katherine has asked for a visit if you can spare a moment before you go." I hung back, smiling politely and discreetly reaching into my purse to see if I'd brought a book to read while I waited. But Edwin grabbed my hand, and we were on our way to Katherine's room.

"She was born in 1925," the church member whispered in the hall. "Turns 100 next December." Her slight frame lay atop the reclining hospital bed like a flower dropped from a bouquet. Her hair shone a crystalline, gleaming white. Her arthritic fingers boasted multiple rings and soft pink polish. Around her neck rested a golden chain with a simple charm that appeared to be from another century. There was a light in her eyes, clear and gracious, a little sad, perhaps, but completely alert, entirely present. Here it was again, the human experience.

I thought of all the things those eyes had seen. I thought of how it must feel to have outlived almost everyone you'd ever known as a young person, to watch them all go. Every surface of her room was lined with pictures of children and teenagers, of grandchildren and great-grandchildren, I assumed. Did they visit? Was she terribly lonely here in this, the twilight of her life?

It quickly became clear that Katherine hadn't asked us there to chat; she had business with my husband, her pastor: She was ready to receive her next mission, to move on from this world, to let go. What strikes me, though, as I remember this sacred moment, is how joyful she seemed. She asked questions about whom she should have her daughter call when she passed; she told Edwin she wanted "The Lord Is My Shepherd" read and

"Great Is Thy Faithfulness" sung at the service. Her tone was smooth, her voice even. She talked as if she were planning a party, her anticipation undampened by the reality that she would not be attending, at least not in the traditional sense.

When logistics were settled, we asked her how she was feeling, what else she needed in the meantime.

That's when it happened. She said she felt "quite alright for now, thank you" and reached across a small table that floated above her bed to grab a large book. "I have my stories."

She gestured to her bookshelf, where I noticed thick, large-print novels by authors I didn't recognize. She pulled something out from under the thin white sheet: her Kindle. "I've got more in here," she said, the corner of her lip turning up slightly in a wry smile. She looked into my eyes, and I felt like we had somehow met before.

Did she know I was an author? That I was struggling to believe my words had purpose, that all this work, this labor to bring my own books into the world, would be worth it?

Before we left, we held her hands—frail, knobbly, and bejeweled—and recited Psalm 23 from the King James Version Bible, just like my own grandmother had taught me. Tears welled in my eyes as we made our way out to the car.

Later, back at my computer, as I write, I think of Katherine's Kindle, the dozen titles on her Murphy bed's shelves, how much comfort she seemed to glean from them. I wish I could remember the names of the authors. I want so much to tell them about the ninety-nine-year-old woman, standing at the outer edge of the human experience, waiting "to let go and let God"—I want to tell those authors that their words were keeping her company. Their creation was a small mercy on that beautiful-terrible Monday in November in that woman's near century of beautiful-terrible days, and perhaps she felt a little less alone because of something they created.

In that moment of tender connection, I saw her books as love letters from God, reminding me—even though I'd never read a word between their binding—that created things have the power to meet us along the road of human experience, to walk us home, to sing a spiritual song of unspoken connection. The song of created things makes us feel a little less afraid in this beautiful-terrible world.

Of the Father's Love Begotten

The first time I read *First Nations Version: An Indigenous Translation of the New Testament*, it sang to something deep within me. One of the many things I love about this translation, written by Native North Americans from over twenty-five tribes, is the poignant names used for the familiar personas of Scripture, translated in the traditional style of storytellers from the Native oral culture. Each name is meant to articulate the essence of the person. God becomes "The Great Spirit," "Giver of Breath," and dozens more. Mary, Mother of God, is called "Bitter Tears," and Moses, "Drawn from the Water." Jesus is "Creator Sets Free." You may have noticed that I was inspired to use some of this translation's names for God throughout this book.

When I first heard Jesus named *Creator Sets Free*, I was confused and intrigued. What did it mean?

Seeing God as a creator, as an artist, is something I dare say I am starting to grasp. I've long known with my head, thanks to the opening of John's gospel, that Jesus was not a mere bystander in creation but one with the Creator from the beginning. Calling Jesus "Creator Sets Free" names this as part of his identity, as something ongoing and essential.

Creating is the most loving thing the Giver of Breath does. (It is right there in the name!) It is from this same love that

Jesus is begotten (born). Christmas, then, that moment when—and here we are at the limits of human language—the Creator becomes also, somehow, the *created*. Christmas means that Jesus, Creator Sets Free, embodies, understands, and redeems the human experience.

The text of "Of the Father's Love Begotten," a lesser-known Christmas carol, was written by Spanish poet Prudentius (350–413 AD) and set to the thirteenth-century Gregorian chant "Divinum Mysterium," first published together in 1582. The text was translated into English by John Mason Neale. That Christmas, after meeting Katherine and her stories, a few days after reading Jesus's new-to-me Indigenous name, I heard "Of the Father's Love Begotten," and realized it was the only song I know that even attempts to sing of these mysteries:

Of the Father's love begotten
ere the worlds began to be,
he is Alpha and Omega,
he the Source, the Ending he,
of the things that are, that have been,
and that future years shall see,
evermore and evermore!

Jesus's life means we have a Creator who knows firsthand the terrible beauty of being human. Intimately, he knew the empty chairs at dining tables, broken relationships, betrayal (Matthew 26:14–16). He set the stars in the sky, and yet he wept with love for his friend when he died (John 11:35). He separated the heavens from the earth and knows end-of-workday weariness (John 4:6). Like Katherine, he watched those he loved go, and he knew what it was to see death coming (Matthew 16:21–23). He felt his mortality deep in his bones, in all its beauty and terror.

His life means we need not be afraid because Jesus, a fellow artist, was born into the beautiful and terrible human experience, and in doing so, just like in creation, he named it as good, named *us* as good. He loved us with his life more than any earthly pastor could; he sets us free.

I like thinking about Jesus as a wild, creative force set free in the world, not coming to condemn us like I feared he would when I was a child, but meeting the raw materials of this broken human experience with joy, patiently shaping them into something more beautiful than terrible; transforming us, like a potter at the wheel, one heart at a time. Unafraid to get his hands dirty, he mixes an artisanal mud concoction to heal a blind man (John 9:6–7) and leans right into the filthy, calloused feet of his disciples (John 13:1–17). A storyteller through and through, his parables (a word from the Greek that means to "come alongside") transcend his time and place like every great work of art and leave us with more questions than answers. The Master of the cosmic cliffhanger, he wrote himself into this play because he loved it, because he loved us, so much.

Jesus's creative work, then, is healing, wholeness.

Isn't that true for every artist?

Jesus is the source of light, in every painting, the light of the world. The darkness cannot overcome it, cannot be extinguished.

We are his poem, his song of delight; he sings us still.

The Babe, the World's Redeemer

When Katherine and I locked eyes, I felt like she grabbed on to a part of me I'd been afraid to release. I hadn't realized how I was white-knuckling the artist life (yet again) until that moment. The angels at Jesus's birth kept telling everyone they meet, "Do not be afraid!" When I stood before Katherine, I heard that command as one specific to me for this moment. I realized I have been giving in to fear, letting it get the best of me: the fear that couldn't do it, write the book I dreamed of writing, sing the song I long to sing, create beauty in spite of the world's brokenness.

I wonder if that's part of what Jesus sets us free from—our fear, from living as a slave to it. I want to create with abandon—this next book, but also this life. I want to write and play and live from a place of unrestrained love, the kind that drives out fear and replaces it with joy.

Jesus sets us free from the lies we have come to believe about ourselves, from other people's stories that we are living. He redeems us from that false sense of ego that tells us we need to be self-sufficient, that success can only be measured in material terms, or the fear that there is not enough—time, talent, energy, resources.

I desperately want, with an artist's eye toward beauty, toward wholeness, to let Jesus redeem the human experience in me once and for all.

Maybe a better question is, what does he set us free *for*?

Let Creation Praise Its Lord

If you find yourself here at the end of this book, weary and wary, cautiously hopeful with a thread of faith as thin as a single page, if you've let fear keep you from creating the things you've always meant to make (this year or evermore), even if you're unsure about this Baby Jesus (by that or any other name), I hope you'll accept this invitation—one I realize I am saying mostly for myself: Do not be afraid.

Instead, may we name each book read from a hospital bed a love letter, each carol sung through tears, a lullaby. Every created thing glows with a recognition of God's creative power fully revealed through Christ, Creator Sets Free. Let us trust that everything made before and since vibrates with the same Love, even the imperfect offerings that come from our very human hands.

This is the call that ignites every burning bush, this is what we are set free for—to trust, to create in love, and to invite others to do the same.

What is creation, what is art, if not the work of setting free? Of being set free? Of overcoming the terror of the world by daring to create beauty anyway?

May it be so. Evermore and evermore.

ARS NOVA

Let Art Set You Free to Create

In *First Nations Version: An Indigenous Translation of the New Testament*, Jesus is named Creator Sets Free. God's creative power is the way God heals and restores this world, which God loves so much.

Create something today that helps you heal and restore the world in whatever small way you can.

Art by others is a spiritual gateway, but you hold within you, whether you are a professional artist or not, the creative power with which God loves and heals the world.

Here is your invitation to connect with the Creator who sets you free.

Make a meal, write a poem, sing your life's song, create a life.

When you create, may you be set free from your fears. May you create beauty in the face of terror and oppression. May you let the light of the world light the way. May you experience the reality that art, creation, is how God loves us.

Coda
What Happens After the End?

> When Jesus saw his mother there, and the disciple whom he loved standing nearby, he said to her, 'Woman, here is your son,' and to the disciple, "Here is your mother." From that time on, this disciple took her into his home.
>
> —John 19:26–28

As a young music student, Form and Analysis class felt like therapy. To untrained ears, it may sound like a Beethoven or Brahms symphony is a free-form composition, for example, but, in reality, every single note can be tucked away into its place in the arc of sonata form. I loved the charts and graphs we'd make explaining each thematic development, every musical gesture or harmonic adventure a composer set out on—it was all there, neat and tidy, in pink and yellow highlighter, from the introduction to the coda. If only life could have such clarity and organization!

Just like in contemporary pop or folk songs—when you're expecting to hear the pattern: verse, chorus, verse, bridge, chorus—classical music has a prescribed design that listeners are waiting for: the return of the main theme. The greats of sonata form—Mozart, Beethoven, Brahms, to name a few—followed suit. Well, mostly.

At a certain point in their compositional output (and for Beethoven, almost right away), the forms were starting to stretch and expand, almost crumble, like an ancient ruin. Suddenly, the coda, which for early composers was just a few extra measures added on at the end, was becoming almost as long as the entire first section, or introducing a brand-new theme altogether. Musicologist James Webster called Beethoven's codas a place for his "new questioning." Endings early on in classicism were neat, quick, tidy. By the coda of Symphony No. 3, I got the sense that Beethoven was searching for the answer to a question we all ask: What happens after the end?

Mary's Coda

I always found it incredible that while dying, Jesus made arrangements for his mother from the cross. He called on his disciple John, the one he loved, and told John to take his mother into his home. "Woman, here is your son," he said to Mary and to the disciple, "Here is your mother" (John 19:26–27).

What happens after the end?

After the worst possible scenario becomes real, after our carefully constructed temples of what is supposed to happen, of wrong and right and up and down, of just and unjust, what happens when they tumble in a blur of blood and grief?

I've often pictured Mary at the cross; it's one of my favorite images in Scripture. I've always felt a kindredness with her. (My grandmother's name was Mary, and one reason my parents named me Merideth was to call me "Meri," as a nod to my father's mother, and—as I chose to believe as a kid—the Mother of God.)

This is the Jesus I love most. The child who loved his mother, the man who, at his moment of greatest pain, thought of her.

I must confess I never thought of what happened to Mary *after* the end. What it must have been like. How she was carried—weeping, no doubt—into a strange place, unsure if there was life after this, most horrible-of-horribles: to give birth to God in the flesh and then to watch him die. As my father says, "No parent should ever outlive their child."

What happens after the end?

Mary's coda happened on the outskirts of Ephesus in modern-day Türkiye.

Temporary Temples

On a sunny morning, toward the end of our Kirk in the Hills Church pilgrimage following in the footsteps of the apostle Paul, we awoke to the news that no spots were left on the Biblical History Tour, and we would not be going. If you've met my husband, Edwin, you know he's nothing if not resourceful. Edwin and I exited our ship, walked past all the dutiful pilgrims boarding tour buses, and found ourselves a yellow cab.

After some haggling about the price, Onur, our driver, agreed to deliver us to Mary's house. We spoke of her like she was a friend we had in common.

Having spent the last five days doing what I was told and following tour guides like Moses, this was new and exhilarating. Onur spoke English well enough and gave us all the history we'd ever wanted. He also offered to deliver us to affordable and trustworthy purveyors of leather, rugs, and other Turkish delights. What more could you ask for?

We climbed and climbed the Mediterranean cliffs in the Yellow-Cab-That-Could, past tangerine, pomegranate, and olive trees, past breathtaking views of the Aegean sea, past what we could make out of the ancient city of Ephesus. Soon, our car stopped. Onur told us he'd meet us at the exit in an hour.

A small stone building stood ahead. Was it a water closet? A souvenir shop? No, it was Mary's last earthly dwelling place.

So this is what happened after the end: this simple home in the most serene place, now a chapel and shrine, bidding both

Christian and Muslim (according to Onur) pilgrims come to pay their respects.

We'd seen and would continue to see so many temples and grand structures in Athens, Ephesus, and Istanbul, temples, mosques, and piles of rocks dedicated to the worship of Artemis and Apollo and every god in between. Mary's house, a peaceful retreat, a humble home hidden in the hills so far from the world she'd known, was, to me, the most beautiful structure of them all.

After you exit the one building—and I cannot reiterate how small it was; it took just a few minutes to walk through—you come upon a stone structure that pilgrims have turned into a prayer wall. Mary's visitors write prayers on small pieces of paper and tie them to strings or stuff them in the holes within the rock.

I tore a page from my journal and bared down on my thigh, scribbling almost illegibly. The pen leaked on my fingers. Endings are not tidy, after all.

Breaking Open

By the time we get to Brahms, a successor of Beethoven, we see that the sonata form wasn't crumbling; it was breaking open. For me, Brahms's most heavenly music appears in the last two minutes of the sonata form, where the coda erupts into a view of paradise itself.

It makes me want to ask you: What if there is more after the end? What if there is something you can only know, create, or say, after you've gotten through, past, the perceived ending? What if, like Brahms, you need to write fifteen minutes of music before the most inspired, genuine, exquisitely beautiful minute and a half of music comes through you? Would the first fifteen minutes be a waste? Of course not. In the end, music theory is just a theory. We put expectations or limitations on God's creative power, his sovereignty over our very form. When we are lost in our development, in the current episode of suffering or trial, we forget that Jesus provided for his mother, the sparrows, and the lilies. What happens after the end? "Where can I go from your Spirit? Where can I flee from your presence?" After the end, there is the coda, and God goes with us, even there.

CODA

What I most want to tell you, here at the end of this book, is that that day in Ephesus, I left a prayer for you. I wrote that everyone who reads these words, everyone who I am privileged to have hold this book, would know that all of creation, from the first theme to the ending chord, is God loving us. That you would know that what happens after the end is that we are not alone.

Even when all seems lost, just as Jesus cared for his mother at the end, God provides for you and for me.

That even when we cannot see how we will get up that mountain or heal from that hurt, God's gentle, humble, upside-down, inside-out kingdom confirms something that Mary knew better than anyone, the main theme of a creative faith—"All things are possible with God."

Think of your name on a small piece of paper inside a wall on a hillside near Ephesus, where Jesus's mother is said to have lived.

There isn't much written or known about her life there, but if she's anything like Beethoven, there were likely many new questions—new blessings, too, no doubt. Even in the codas of life, God is still creating, still loving us.

Sometimes what we perceive as the end is just the beginning.

Ars Nova
Creative Creed

Let Art Be a Spiritual Gateway

Naming what we believe helps us shine the light of faith into the darkest corners of the world. Spiritual communities and groups of faith have been writing creeds and confessions for millennia to proclaim what they believe to be true, unite communities across time, and foster a strong sense of identity.

Having read this book, what do you believe about the nature of the universe? What is the power of art? What is true about God? Create your own creative creed as an act of celebration and worship.

Here's mine:

I believe there is an Ultimate Reality, a Maker, a Great Spirit, a Giver of Breath, an Artist, that exists outside of gender and has been revealed to me as the triune God of Abraham, Isaac, and Jacob, of Sarah, Hagar, and Rebekah—three in one—Father, Son, and Holy Spirit.

I believe the spark of Love that set all life in motion lives within me like a secret pilot light, that creation continues through even me.

I believe that when Ultimate Reality breaks through, it is a melody we recognize, that it meets us where we are, in our shame and sadness, in our brokenness or stubborn joy, that it reminds us: We are created to create.

I believe that ART is not defined by special skill or elitist craft, that no human life is excluded from God's creative love, our Maker's fingerprints can be found on every creation, and that everyone creating a life is an artist.

I believe in the God who sees like only an artist can, beholding us like van Gogh's mysterious olive trees. We are found worthy of returning to, again and again. We are made new in every subtle shift of light, in every new season.

I believe in the gifts hidden within the chaos of creation, which by grace we get to order alongside God. We can mend the broken with what we have—even when all we have are LEGO.

I believe that art, and therefore life, is messy; the Holy Spirit is as much wild goose as angelic dove, that every unexpected detour is ripe with creative possibility.

I believe that God speaks through created things—that listening is *the work*. In the battlefields of life, we can "be still and know," because, like God did for Brahms, the Giver of Breath sends songs across the valleys, the chasms, of our fear and scarcity.

I believe that when we show up, rugged and imperfect and persistent, weary and wanting, when we reach for the hem of His garment, when we hang on to the threads of our creative callings, we find God hanging on to us—a love that won't let go.

I believe that creation is an ongoing process. Like Gaudí's Basílica de la Sagrada Família, God is still working beyond what we may see in our lifetime. God has embedded our Maker's image within us, like a great architect, who, as C. S. Lewis says, "is building a palace . . . He intends to come and live in it Himself."

I believe that our Great Composer knows our tune's truest name. It is *the* gift to be simple, *the* gift to be free, to walk from the shadows of our narrow, limited dreams and step into a deeper calling that is about more than only us.

I believe in the power of art to be a burning bush, to remind us that human life should never be consumed or appropriated, but God loving us like only an artist can, means our Creator collects our tears in a bottle like precious artifacts.

I believe that it is through creation that our Maker "works righteousness and justice for all the oppressed" (Psalm 103:6) and invites us into the van, to join God's mission toward wholeness and healing for all.

I believe that God is my clay sculptor, who never stops forming and reforming my heart, drawing me into transformation and sanctification, not in my tidy timeline but in a spiral of "with-ness."

With God, I believe it is safe to lament, to weep, to be myself as I am made. I choose to be in relationship with my Creator even when I don't understand God's silence, even when my questions go unanswered.

I believe that life is a long let-go; I can release everything I cherish into God's hands. I know that everything I have is God's. My Maker has loved my loves longer and more completely than I ever could.

I believe that sometimes, in lieu of flowers, God sends a river. Christ is the wisdom of the universe, whispered in the questions of creation; an all-at-once particular and universal gift that makes every sunset personally painted for me.

I believe that when we "Serve the Gift," God sets about the work of making hearts pure again, bringing a new creation into the here and now. When we are willing to say yes when asked to dance, the Giver of Breath leads us. What Bach wrote in the margin of his Bible is true: "Where there is devotional music, God is present with his grace."

I have asked, "Am I good enough?" And I've heard Jesus answer with a mirth as boundless as creation itself: "I AM."

I have seen, in the frames of old pictures, God loving me in each moment, sensing God's presence in both the painful junctures and the brightest flashes of joy.

I believe that God's word—the histories, poems, and parables of the Bible—reveals our Maker's character as an Artist writing one epic creation story. Beginning with creation in Genesis and ending with new creation in Revelation, God's creative power is synonymous with God's love.

I believe I am a poem my Maker is still writing, created not out of necessity, but love. Not some form of technology designed for production, but a poem whose strength stems from tenderness. I believe that work doesn't make me free, that love does—that this epoch God is crafting with its twists and turns is our Artist naming this beautiful and terrible human experience holy. Jesus is God loving us with God's life. He was there at the beginning, our Creator Sets Free.

May you see that this book, this day, this breath, and the next, are God hoping with God's hands, healing the world God loves so much through the sacred beauty of created things—through ART.

Art is how God loves us, but also how we love.

Therefore, go in peace to make a life, believing you are God's painting, God's song, a tender mound of clay, the work of a Creator's hands, a poem, a unique and beloved masterpiece. The real work of art is the person you are becoming, the person God created you to be in love.

Ordinary things are given meaning because of who they belong to, and you belong to God. You needn't hide anything about yourself to belong; there is nothing to earn. God made you and loves you like only an artist can.

May the source of all goodness scatter the shadows of your shame.

May every note in the aria that is your life become a Word of God, every work of art you encounter be a love letter from Love itself.

May the Maker of words and worlds remind you when you doubt: Your words matter.

May God give you courage to steal the pencil, to be a flowering onion, to read your name in the Book of Life, to walk on water, to move unfettered among the stars.

May you allow yourself to shine with the spark of a divine and infinite love, a mirror in a mirror in a mirror . . .

Acknowledgments

When you look closely at the thread of this book's message, you'll notice it is not one single piece of string but a multilayered cord of meaning and effort that came together with the help of many people. I am eternally grateful to get to do this work and for all those who made it possible.

To my dear friend, Mara Eller, who read and edited the earliest versions of almost all these writings. This book, Mara, in its very structure and spirit, owes so much to your steadfast support and invaluable insight.

To my literary agent and friend in the faith, Don Pape: Thank you for seeing the potential in this book's message and for your persistent efforts in finding it the perfect home.

To my editor, Lisa Kloskin, and the whole crew at Broadleaf: You believed in this book and trusted me to write it. I am grateful!

To Amy Davis, a tireless advocate and friend to those caught in human trafficking: Your initial insights on "Art is a Burning Bush" were invaluable in helping me articulate the complex realities of life on the streets for trafficked women.

To Heather Lanier, a fellow poet and clergy spouse, who helped with some early editing of the poems in this collection and who was the first to introduce me to Father John Keating's work and the "Eight Agreements of the Snowmass Interreligious Conference." I am grateful for your support and camaraderie in this writer life.

To our entire church family at Kirk in the Hills Presbyterian Church (PCUSA) in Bloomfield Hills, Michigan, especially my small group ladies—Sarah Ford, Gloria Chon, Lauren Clopton, Claire Devlin, and Julie Webb—who helped me read the Bible with new eyes. (Reader: Find yourself a group that helps you wrestle with Scripture!) The love and support of our entire faith community at the Kirk have strengthened my faith and made this book possible.

My sincere gratitude to those who help me find time to create, including our dedicated babysitters, especially Jasmine Pittenger and Amy Schwarb, who gave me the gift of time.

To my incredible parents, Deb and Tommy: Thank you for instilling in me the values of perseverance and hard work, and for believing in my crazy dreams. To my siblings, Heather, Tombo, and Mack, thank you for the laughter, the perspective, and for always being a source of unwavering support. And to my dear mother-in-love, Azucena Estevez, for all the delicious meals and selfless care you give to all of us. The love and encouragement of these people have made this book possible.

To my two favorite creations, Eva and Eli: Thank you for sleeping until 7:00 a.m. (most days) so I could write this book. You remind me that art and life are messy, and I love your mess more than anyone else's. Your faith in our Maker and your creative joy inspire me.

To my love, Edwin, for helping me serve my gifts, for making me laugh, and for calling me into a deeper faith and love for Jesus. Sunset Alert!

Soli Deo Gloria.

Study Guide

Philosopher and education reformer John Dewey's work is often summarized as: "We don't learn by experience, we learn by reflecting on experience." These questions are designed to help you reflect on the experience of reading this book, to go deeper into art as a spiritual gateway to God.

While these can be done independently, coming together to discuss art—and specifically the intersection of art and spirituality—is a profound experience in community. Since 2017, I have been leading online and in-person creative cluster groups with artists from a variety of backgrounds and faith expressions. We have stumbled around in the dark for words to share our experience of the spiritual, even though we express Ultimate Reality in many different ways. I have learned so much about my own faith by encountering those whose expressions differ from mine, and my hope with this guide is to offer a starting point for readers, wherever they stand on their path of faith.

Each section offers a few short questions for those who are exploring their beliefs, Seekers, and Christian readers, corresponding to each chapter. The discussion questions for each chapter begin as open and expansive as possible and become more specifically Christian. I hope you will use whatever sparks conversation for you or the group gathered.

For those seeking a more in-depth study of Christian Holy Scripture, the final question of each chapter's list invites a deeper reflection on the biblical texts mentioned, with specific invitations to delve further through the lens of art. Holy Scripture is a work of art itself, and so I encourage you to explore whatever translation helps you enter into the texts' meaning most deeply.

For book clubs and small groups, I recommend reading the chapter, viewing or listening to the work of art it is based on, and attempting the Ars Nova exercise on your own before each meeting. The book would easily fit into thirteen weeks or the length of a semester. Designate a notebook to collect your impressions so you can have them ready to share. When you gather, after a brief prayer or opening ritual (such as lighting a candle, ringing a bell, or enjoying a moment of silence), view or experience the art from the chapter together again. Use the QR code in the back for a curated list of all the art discussed in this book. Explore the questions, and close the gathering with another ritual, such as a prayer or a simple song.

Introduction and Prelude: Chopin, *Andante Spianato*:

1. *Art is How God Loves Us* is a record of moments, "an invitation to experience this love of Ultimate Reality, through both sacred and secular, God and human-created things: art." Share a time when you have felt the presence of an Ultimate Reality through art.
2. What words do you use to describe "Ultimate Reality" in your life?
3. When have you stood before something real, "after hearing of its rumors for years?" What was the experience like?
4. How would you define the words "art" and "artist"? Redefining ART as *Atoms Responding to Transcendence*, disconnecting the practice of creation from specialty skill or performance—how does this open your definition? If you believed that art and artistry were not part of an exclusive club for trained professionals, would your life change? How?

5. At the end of the prelude, there is a short reference from Isaiah 42:3: "a bruised reed he will not break, and a dimly burning wick he will not quench; he will faithfully bring forth justice." This verse comes from a section of Isaiah called "The Suffering Servant," which Christians believe prophesies of Jesus.
   a. Read Isaiah 42:1–9. What words or phrases stick out?
   b. When have you felt like a "bruised reed" or a "dimly burning wick"?
   c. What is the good news in this passage for you?

Chapter 1: Vincent van Gogh, *Olive Trees*

1. How do you relate to a higher power? C. S. Lewis offers the playwright metaphor: What lenses color the way you see God?
2. "How is the way you view God serving your creative expansion?" (Julia Cameron) Has your "God Concept" changed throughout your life? If so, how?
3. Consider God as an Artist. What new insights color your faith experience through that lens?
4. "Art is the highest form of hope." Do you agree? How do you feel when you consider God is "hoping with God's hands" by creating you?
5. In Genesis 16:13, Sarai's servant Hagar flees from the brokenness of her situation and encounters the holy. "So she named the Lord who spoke to her, 'You are El-roi,' (the God who sees) for she said, 'Have I really seen God and remained alive after seeing him?'"
   a. When have you felt seen by God?
   b. Take a moment to see yourself through God's eyes. If God loved you like van Gogh's Olive Trees, how

does this change the way you approach your own idiosyncrasies or brokenness?
   c. If you believe "the Artist God loves you enough to paint another and then another iteration," what iteration of you is emerging now? How are you being called to change, to be more like Jesus?

Chapter 2: Jan Vormann, *Dispatchwork*

1. What kinds of chaos make you feel most uncomfortable?
2. What areas of your life feel most chaotic?
3. Share or write about a time when things had to fall apart to fall together.
4. Have you ever felt God invite you to "pull all the contents of the cabinet out onto the counter to air out"? Have you found being honest and vulnerable in prayer to be healing? What do you need to be more honest about now?
5. The creation narrative is woven throughout the book as a whole. Take the time now to read Genesis 1 closely.
   a. What stands out to you this time?
   b. How does the fact that God orders the chaos impact the way you treat your home? Your mess? Your children or those in your care?
   c. What is God teaching you now?

Chapter 3: Johannes Brahms, Symphony No. 1

1. Brahms was known to burn the scores that he felt weren't worthy of human eyes. Have you ever felt frustrated or ashamed of something you created? What did that feel like?

2. What do you do when you feel stuck?
3. If "listening is the work," what work are you tempted to do in lieu of listening?
4. Has God ever spoken to you in flowers or birdsong? If not nature, what other ways have you received inspiration or clarity?
5. Read Psalm 46:
   a. What battles are you fighting in your life right now?
   b. Remember a time of trouble when God felt ever-present. How does this memory affirm the truths of the psalmist's words?
   c. What is harder for you, being still or knowing God is God?
   d. Name some practical ways you could "be still and know," listening for God's voice over the noise and chaos of life.

Chapter 4: Antoni Gaudí, Basílica de la Sagrada Família

1. Do you have your own version of "pianos in the terminal"? What things in life seem joyful to everyone else, but bring feelings of dread or shame in you? Write about one of them and share the response with someone you trust.
2. Do you choose a word of the year? How do you set your intentions and expectations for each season of life?
3. In this chapter, I name how close proximity with my family impacted our intimacy and deepened our connection quickly. Who are you closest to in proximity? With whom do you spend most of your *quantity* time? How does this impact your connection to those you love most?

4. How would you practically apply this idea of hanging on to the thread in your life in general? How do you keep what is most important at the front of your mind? Make a list of ideas for quieting the noise and staying focused on what matters most.
5. In this chapter, there is a story of Eva holding on to the back of my sweater. This is a nod to a Gospel story found in Matthew 9:20–22. This passage recounts the account of a woman who had been suffering from bleeding for twelve years, who believed that if she only touched the hem of Jesus's garment, she would be healed.
   a. Read Matthew 9:20–22.
   b. What suffering do you long for Jesus to heal in you?
   c. What traits or qualities did the woman have that made her believe and fight through the crowd to touch Jesus's garment?
   d. What would healing and wholeness look like for you today? Turn your answers into a prayer.

Chapter 5: Joseph Brackett, "Simple Gifts"

1. Have you ever lived "across the street from your dream," out of fear? What do you think is the solution to walking from the shadows of fear into the light?
2. What are some names you have gone by in your life? What feelings or roles go along with each name? Which name feels most like your true self?
3. The lyrics to the Shaker tune are: "'Tis the gift to be simple, 'tis the gift to be free." Reflect on when simplicity and freedom have gone together in your life.

4. Has anyone in your life ever "rejoiced over you with singing"? Write or share about a memory if you have one.
5. The Scriptures from this chapter were all iterations of God singing throughout Scripture. Read Zephaniah 3:17, Job 38:7, and Matthew 26:30.
   a. How do these examples of the melodic heart of God differ from one another?
   b. Which one resonates with you most?
   c. If you had to imagine your truest self as a melody to be sung by the heart of God in creation, how would you describe it?
   d. What is God teaching you through these metaphors?

Chapter 6: Faith Ringgold, "Picasso's Studio"

1. What makes you feel free?
2. Reflect on a time when you have been at "the margins," serving those in need or being served. What did you learn about yourself through that experience?
3. Seeing art creation through the lens of the burning bush is empowering, inviting us to remember the cry of the oppressed. In your opinion, what role does art play in revolution and protest?
4. Through "Picasso's Studio" and other quilts from her work in the *French Collection*, Ringgold imagines conversations with art history greats, rewriting the often-harmful narratives against women and artists of color. What narratives from your own history need rewriting? How could art play a role?
5. Read Exodus 3:1–15

   a. What might God be calling you to "turn aside to see" in your life today?
   b. Have you "heard" God speak to you? Reflect on the experience.
   c. God discloses God's name in Exodus 14: "I am who I am." What does this name represent for you? How does this name speak into God's creative work that began in creation and continues today?
   d. What mission is God calling you to today?

Chapter 7: Ruth Duckworth, *The Creation*

1. The image of our "selves" fitting inside each other like a nesting doll is from poet Maggie Smith. Take a moment to list a few different iterations of yourself that you've witnessed change and grow in your lifetime. How is the person you are now different from each of them?
2. How has art helped you in times of suffering?
3. What do you think creating art in concentration camps provided for the prisoners?
4. Take this quote from clay sculptor Ruth Duckworth: "I think of life as a unity. This includes mountains, mice, rocks, trees, women, and men. It's all one big lump of clay." Have you sensed the unity of all things? If so, when?
5. Read Isaiah 64:8 and Jeremiah 18:1–7.
   a. Reflect on what you feel the metaphor of God as a potter means to you.
   b. How have you felt God reshaping you in your life?
   c. In both Isaiah and Jeremiah, there is lament. How does the fact that God goes with us in our suffering and despair, the fact that roughly 40 percent

of the psalms are those of lament, what aspect of God's character is on display in those passages?

   d. Read Elie Wiesel's "Prayer for the Days of Awe." Have you ever been "divorced" from God? If so, what helped you find your way back? If you are currently, may you pray with complete honesty, if or when you feel ready, knowing God can hold our lamentation and anger.

Chapter 8: Arvo Pärt, "Spiegel im Spiegel"

1. Do you connect certain life events with certain music? What songs come to mind when you remember the best and hardest days of your life?
2. What areas of your life do you tend to hold too tightly? Name the specific fears behind the death grip.
3. Reflect on a time when you let go of a person or situation. What was hardest about it? Were your fears realized?
4. Maybe you noticed that chapter 4 (Hang On to the Thread) and chapter 8 (Let Go, Let Go, Let Go) are, at first glance, contradictory. Do we need to hang on or let go? Are there specific seasons or circumstances that call for one and not the other? How do we know which to do when? Explore this dissonance in your journal or in the group gathered.
5. Read 1 Corinthians 13:4–13.
   a. What role does control play in the love described in 1 Corinthians 13?
   b. "God knows the ache of open hands." What does this line mean to you?
   c. "God doesn't ask us by our own strength or strong moral character to be patient or kind, to not boast

or never fail." Are you tempted to earn love in this way? How does your heart open when you consider that the chapter from Corinthians is not prescriptive, but descriptive?

   d. What is something new that God is teaching you through this familiar Scripture today?

Chapter 9: Christi Belcourt, *Wisdom of the Universe*

1. Have you ever felt that nature was a consolation in times of grief? How has nature been a companion along life's journey?
2. What does wisdom mean to you, and how do you go about growing in wisdom in your life?
3. In what ways can you contribute to the "healing" of the world that Belcourt describes?
4. Have you ever felt like a work of art was made just for you? If so, which one?
5. Read through some of the Scriptures that personify creation: Psalm 19, Psalm 98, Romans 8, etc.
   a. What is creation doing in these passages, and what do you believe this says about God?
   b. Why do you think Jesus asked so many questions to those he encountered?
   c. What is God teaching you through these questions of Jesus?
      i. Matthew 16:15: "Who do you say that I am?"
      ii. Matthew 16:26: "What good will it be for a man if he gains the whole world, yet forfeits his soul?"
      iii. Matthew 7:9: "Which of you, if his son asks for bread, will give him a stone?"
      iv. John 5:6: "Do you want to be made well?"

   d. In John 12:32, Jesus says, "And I, when I am lifted up from the earth, will draw all people to myself." When have you felt Jesus draw you near to him?

Chapter 10: J. S. Bach, "Mache dich, mein Herze rein" from *St Matthew Passion*

1. If your heart feels less than pure, what does it feel like? Examples: weary, lost, broken, shameful, fearful.
2. What talents or gifts were you given? Are you "serving the work," or are you seeking to make the work serve you?
3. How do you respond when you feel you aren't talented enough? What feelings come up when you consider the limits of your abilities?
4. Are faith and creativity intertwined for you?
5. Read Psalm 51 and 2 Chronicles 5 as if they were stories of a loved one, listening for God's character to be revealed.
   a. What lines stick out to you in Psalm 51? Read 2 Samuel 11–12 to remind yourself what David was seeking repentance for. Does anything surprise you about David's boldness in this psalm? If so, what?
   b. When you ask yourself if you're "good enough," what would it mean to hear Jesus answer, "I am"?
   c. 2 Chronicles 5:13 says, "The temple of the Lord was filled with the cloud, and the priests could not perform their service." And next to this verse, J. S. Bach wrote, "In devotional music, God is present with his grace." Does your "service" feel devotional? What could you shift about your practice to experience the presence of God's grace?

d. "He is good; his love endures forever" is a refrain that appears throughout the Bible. In Psalm 136, it appears 26 times. What's essential about this truth? What does it feel like to repeat it so often? What is God teaching you about it now?

Chapter 11: Billy Collins, "Introduction to Poetry"

1. Does the idea of a "portfolio career" resonate with you? What different aspects of your life do you put energy toward? List them. Is anything missing?
2. How would you define a "joy-filled life," and what role does creativity or art play in that?
3. Does anything feel unsustainable about your life now? Reflect on what might need to change.
4. In which activities or aspects of life do you feel most like *techne* (needed for usefulness, capability, or productivity), and when do you feel like *poiēma* (loved for beauty, design, or connection)?
5. Read Ephesians 2. Look up verse 10 in a few different translations, watching for how the word for "masterpiece, artwork, creation" is translated differently.
   a. What is the context for verse 10? What do you think Paul wants us to know about how God loves us?
   b. Does the fact that you are God's beloved creation change the way you see your weaknesses and strengths? If so, how?
   c. What do you believe the good work that God has "ordained for you beforehand" is?

Chapter 12: Aurelius Prudentius/John Mason Neale, *Of the Father's Love Begotten*

1. What does the phrase "the human experience" mean to you? How have you felt especially human lately?
2. What works of art have kept you company, walked you home? Has art ever felt like a "love letter from God"?
3. Where have you experienced the "whiplash of joy and pain, of malignancy and miracle" in your own life?
4. Who are the people you attempt to "love with your life?"
5. Compare John 1 from the First Nations Translation with another more common translation.
   a. What differences do you find? What phrases stick out to you now? What is God teaching you?
   b. The First Nations Translation names Jesus "Creator Sets Free." What does this name mean to you? How might it speak to God's character in a new way?
   c. The three parts of the book explore different iterations of light, or the absence thereof—spark, shadow, and source. Reflecting on these three iterations of light, which do you find most prevalent in your current spiritual journey, and how does John's proclamation influence your perspective on that?
   d. What does it mean to you to "be set free"? What do you want to be set free from, and what do you want to be set free for?

Coda: What Happens After the End?

1. How do you handle endings? What feelings come up for you? Name whatever is here now as you finish this book.
2. If your life had an original theme or a deep truth that kept returning, what would it be?
3. Have you ever experienced a "coda" in life, a time after a significant event that brought new questions or blessings?
4. In the coda, I share, "This is the Jesus I love most. The child who loved his mother, the man who, at his moment of greatest pain, thought of her." What is your "favorite Jesus" in the Gospels?
5. Read John 19:26–28
   a. What does this story from the end of Jesus's life reveal about his character? God's?
   b. As you finish this book, what is God teaching you?

Notes

Introduction: Art's Open Door

xi ***fixed or movable "do" are two different ways of teaching solfège:*** Put simply: "Fixed do" means the note C is always "do," whereas "movable do" means the "do" changes based on whatever key you are in.

xiii ***a group of religious and spiritual contemplatives:*** Netanel Miles-Yepez and Ken Wilber, *The Common Heart: An Experience of Interreligious Dialogue* (Shambhala Publications, 2002).

xv ***"thick skin, tender-hearted":*** Rachel Held Evans with Jeff Chu, *Wholehearted Faith: Embracing Joy, Belonging, and Hope When Life Doesn't Go as Planned* (HarperOne, 2021).

xviii ***I heard a story once about a pastor:*** W. R. Moody, *The Life of D. L. Moody* (Fleming H. Revell, 1900), 149.

xix ***Anne Lamott's conversion story:*** Anne Lamott, *Traveling Mercies: Some Thoughts on Faith* (Anchor Books, 2000), 44–55.

xix ***"God creates out of love, not necessity":*** Makoto Fujimura, *Art and Faith: A Theology of Making* (Yale University Press, 2021), 17.

xix ***a story of a spiritual experience she had at the Met Museum:*** Sarah Bessey, *Field Notes for the Wilderness: Practices for an Evolving Faith* (Convergent Books, 2024), 106–7.

xxii ***My faith has always felt more like a trampoline than a brick wall:*** Rob Bell, *Velvet Elvis: Repainting the Christian Faith* (Zondervan, 2005).

Prelude: Redefining Art

xxx ***"already and not yet":*** Geerhardus Vos, *The Pauline Eschatology* (P&R Publishing, 1994).

Part I: Spark

2 ***after David Whyte's poem "Self-Portrait":*** David Whyte, "Self-Portrait," in *River Flow: New & Selected Poems, 1984–2007* (Many Rivers Press, 2007).

Chapter 1: The Artist Sees

5 ***C. S. Lewis fielded questions about whether we would encounter God in space:*** C. S. Lewis, "The Seeing Eye," in *Christian Reflections*, ed. Walter Hooper (Eerdmans, 1995), 171.

6 ***"How is the way you view God serving your creative expansion?"*** Julia Cameron, *The Artist's Way: A Spiritual Path to Higher Creativity* (Jeremy P. Tarcher, 1992), 191.

7 ***he gave him more lines than any other character:*** "Has anyone published a line count of Shakespearean roles? What are the top 10?" *The Guardian*, online query, https://tinyurl.com/3hw2tx9t.

7 ***"Art is the highest form of hope.":*** *Art Is the Highest Form of Hope & Other Quotes by Artists* (Phaidon Press, 2016). Or Gerhard Richter, "Text," in *Documenta 7: Katalog*, edited by Rudi Fuchs et al. (D & V, 1982).

8 ***In a letter to his brother Theo:*** "Letter from Vincent van Gogh to Theo van Gogh, Saint-Rémy, 28 September 1889," *van Gogh's Letters*, accessed September 16, 2025, https://www.webexhibits.org/vangogh/letter/20/608.htm

9 ***In Celtic spirituality, this was named the "original blessing.":*** Mary C. Earle, *Celtic Christian Spirituality: Essential Writings Annotated & Explained* (SkyLight Paths, 2011).

Chapter 2: Order the Chaos

14 ***With a quick internet search, I learned about Dispatchwork:*** See https://www.dispatchwork.info/.

16 ***"black trash bag energy":*** Kendra Adachi, *The PLAN: Manage Your Time Like a Lazy Genius* (Convergent Books, 2024).

19 ***In Celtic spirituality, the Spirit is often depicted as a wild graylag goose:*** John O'Donohue, *Anam Cara: A Book of Celtic Wisdom* (HarperPerennial, 1997).

Chapter 3: Listening Is the Work

25 ***"anxiety of influence":*** Mark Evan Bonds, *After Beethoven: Imperatives of Originality in the Symphony* (Harvard University Press, 1996).

26 ***"the manuscript of the first movement of the symphony is marked as "lost":*** See Johannes Brahms, *Symphony no. 1 in C minor, op. 68: autograph manuscript, 1876 Sept.*, The Morgan Library & Museum, accessed May 28, 2025, https://www.themorgan.org/music-manuscripts-and-printed-music/114285.

26 ***"what Ira Glass calls "the Gap":*** Mike Birbiglia, host, *Mike Birbiglia's Working It Out*, podcast, episode 100, "Ira Glass Part 3: The Best Advice," Apple Podcasts, June 5, 2023, https://podcasts.apple.com/us/podcast/100-ira-glass-part-3-the-best-advice/id1515419751?i=1000615659194.

31 ***As Ingrid Gott-Maidoff says:*** Ingrid Goff-Maidoff, *What Holds Us: New and Selected Poems* (Sarah's Circle, 2011), 43.

32 ***originating with the Desert Mothers and Fathers:*** Enzo Bianchi, *Lectio Divina: From God's Word to Our Lives* (Paraclete Press, 2015).

Chapter 5: Shadow Careers and Simple Gifts

49 ***Professor J:*** Name has been changed.

50 ***"shadow careers":*** Steven Pressfield, *Turning Pro: Tap Your Inner Power and Create Your Life's Work* (Black Irish Entertainment, 2012), 12.

58 ***what sociologist Martha Beck calls your "Essential Self,":*** Martha Beck, *Finding Your Own North Star: Claiming the Life You Were Meant to Live* (Harmony Books, 2002), 38.

Chapter 6: Art Is a Burning Bush

60 ***Nan:*** Name has been changed.

61 ***with a known human trafficking problem:*** At the time of this writing, Michigan is ranked seventh in the United States for these crimes. With Detroit's Canadian border, a popular smuggling spot, and the sprawling abandoned lots left after the economic crash of 2008, the drug dealers and traffickers squat throughout the depressing,

dilapidated homes. Over 16,554 Michigan victims reported abuse to the U.S. National Human Trafficking Hotline in 2021. Read more harrowing statistics here: https://tinyurl.com/yz2b67jr.

64 ***TJ:*** Name has been changed.

66 ***In the handwritten letter to her aunt that flanks the quilt's edges:*** Faith Ringgold, *Dancing at the Louvre: Faith Ringgold's French Collection and Other Story Quilts* (University of California Press, 1998), 33.

68 ***Willia's aunt answers her many questions about the power of art:*** Ringgold, *Dancing at the Louvre*, 4.

Chapter 7: Clay Sculptor

75 ***like one of those ceramic nesting dolls:*** This image was introduced to me by Maggie Smith, *You Could Make This Place Beautiful* (Atria/One Signal, 2024), 7.

83 ***"Auschwitz must and will forever remain a question mark only . . .":*** Elie Wiesel, "A Prayer for the Days of Awe," *New York Times*, October 2, 1997, accessed May 28, 2025, https://www.nytimes.com/1997/10/02/opinion/a-prayer-for-the-days-of-awe.html.

Chapter 8: Let Go, Let Go, Let Go

98 ***the distortion of disordered love:*** Augustine, *Confessions*, trans. Henry Chadwick (Oxford University Press, 1991).

98 ***I wrote a whole book about:*** Merideth Hite Estevez, *The Artist's Joy* (Broadleaf Books, 2024).

102 ***this exercise was inspired by Julia Cameron's The Artist's Way:*** Julia Cameron, *The Artist's Way: A Spiritual Path to Higher Creativity* (Jeremy P. Tarcher, 1992).

Part III: Source

103 ***"feeds the lake":*** Madeleine L'Engle, *Walking on Water: Reflections on Faith and Art* (Harold Shaw, 1980), 13.

104 ***remembering how to walk on water:*** L'Engle, *Walking on Water.*

104 ***Art, like all of life, is not a timeline but a spiral:*** C. S. Lewis, *The Last Battle* (HarperCollins, 2025).

Chapter 9: The Particular and Universal Wisdom of Created Things

107 ***some say the Cuyahoga River was named after an Indigenous word meaning "crooked":*** "Cuyahoga River," Ohio Department of Natural Resources, Ohio.gov, n.d., accessed May 30, 2025, https://www.epa.gov/great-lakes-aocs/cuyahoga-river-aoc.

108 ***"All species, the lands, the waters are one beating organism . . .":*** Christi Belcourt, "Artist's statement: Christi Belcourt on *The Wisdom of the Universe*," *AGO Insider*, August 7, 2014, https://ago.ca/agoinsider/artists-statement-christi-belcourt-wisdom-universe.

109 ***Hobart says these wise words about the power of the painting:*** Donna Tartt, *The Goldfinch* (Little, Brown, 2013), 758–59.

112 ***God's all-powerful grace pulls the threads of the universe together:*** Karl Barth, *Church Dogmatics*, trans. G. W. Bromiley and T. F. Torrance. 14 vols. (T&T Clark, 1936–1975).

115 ***"God's particularity":*** Barth, *Church Dogmatics*.

115 ***"right now and not yet":*** Barth, *Church Dogmatics*.

Chapter 10: The Gospel According to Bach

122 ***"Cast your deadly doing down":*** From the hymn "It is Finished!" by James Proctor.

124 ***another perspective, shifting our focus from performance to collaboration:*** L'Engle, *Walking on Water*, 13.

127 "***where there is devotional music, God is always present with his grace":*** Johann Sebastian Bach, *J.S. Bach's Personal Copy of Abraham Calov's Bible Commentary: The Bach Bible: Facsimile Edition with Transcriptions and English Translations of Bach's Annotations*, ed. Albert Clement (Uitgeverij Van Wijnen, 2017).

128 ***that performance began the Bach renaissance:*** Christoph Wolff, *Johann Sebastian Bach: The Learned Musician* (W. W. Norton, 2000).

130 ***"Getting out of the way and listening is not something that comes easily . . .":*** L'Engle, *Walking on Water*.

131 ***the arc of the universe is long:*** The quote "the arc of the universe is long and bends towards justice," is attributed to Martin Luther King Jr., but it was actually a paraphrase of a sermon by Theodore Parker entitled "Of Justice and the Conscience," published in *Ten Sermons of Religion* (Boston: Crosby, Nichols, and Company, 1853), 1–30.

132 ***"For the past eighty years I have started each day in the same manner . . .":*** Pablo Casals and Albert E. Kahn, *Joys and Sorrows: Reflections by Pablo Casals As Told to Albert E. Kahn* (Simon and Schuster, 1970).

Chapter 11: Portfolio Life

142 ***"I ask them to take a poem . . .":*** Billy Collins, "Introduction to Poetry" in *The Apple that Astonished Paris* (University of Arkansas Press, 1996). Copyright © 1988, 1996 by Billy Collins.

144 ***stumbling around in the dark is a spiritual practice:*** Barbara Brown Taylor, *Learning to Walk in the Dark* (HarperOne, 2014).

145 ***"Metaphor is the only language we have to speak of God":*** Rich Roll, host, *The Rich Roll Podcast*, episode 788, October 19, 2023, "Pete Holmes . . . is Not for Everyone", www.richroll.com/podcast/pete-holmes-788/.

Chapter 12: Creator Sets Free

150 ***"Here is the world . . .":*** Frederick Buechner, *Beyond Words: Daily Readings in the ABC's of Faith* (HarperCollins, 2004), 138.

151 ***Katherine has asked for a visit:*** Name has been changed.

Ars Nova: Creative Creed

166 ***"is building a palace . . . He intends to come and live in it Himself":*** C. S. Lewis, *Mere Christianity* (Touchstone, 1996), 175.

169 ***to walk on water:*** L'Engle, *Walking on Water*, 47.

Study Guide

173 ***"We don't learn by experience, we learn by reflecting on experience":*** While this quote does not appear directly in the published writings of Dewey, it is often attributed to him and provides a succinct paraphrase for the philosophy laid out in John Dewey, *How We Think: A Restatement of the Relation of Reflective Thinking to the Educative Process* (D.C. Heath, 1933).

Featured Works of Art

Frédéric Chopin, *Andante spianato Op. 22* (1834)
Vincent van Gogh, *Olive Trees* (1889)
Jan Vormann, *Dispatchwork* (2007—ongoing)
Johannes Brahms, Symphony No. 1 (completed 1876)
Antoni Gaudí, Basílica de la Sagrada Família (construction began in 1882, ongoing)
Joseph Brackett Jr., "Simple Gifts" (1848)
Faith Ringgold, "Picasso's Studio" from *The French Collection* (1991)
Ruth Duckworth, *The Creation* (1984)
Arvo Pärt, "Spiegel im Spiegel" (1978)
Christi Belcourt, *Wisdom of the Universe* (2014)
J. S. Bach, "Mache dich, mein Herze rein" from *St Matthew Passion* (1727)
Billy Collins, "Introduction to Poetry" (1988)
Aurelius Prudentius/John Mason Neale, "Of the Father's Love Begotten" (Original Latin: c. 348–413 AD; Published: 1582; English translation: 1851)

Access images and recordings of the art featured in this book at artistsforjoy.org/art or scan the QR code below.

www.ingramcontent.com/pod-product-compliance
Ingram Content Group UK Ltd.
Pitfield, Milton Keynes, MK11 3LW, UK
UKHW012054010726
472576UK00007B/21/J

9 798889 836452